The Pastoral

by
JOHN HEATH-STUBBS

OXFORD UNIVERSITY PRESS
1969

Oxford University Press, Ely House, London W.1

GLASGOW   NEW YORK   TORONTO   MELBOURNE   WELLINGTON
CAPE TOWN   SALISBURY   IBADAN   NAIROBI   LUSAKA   ADDIS ABABA
BOMBAY   CALCUTTA   MADRAS   KARACHI   LAHORE   DACCA
KUALA LUMPUR   SINGAPORE   HONG KONG   TOKYO

© JOHN HEATH-STUBBS 1969

FILMSET AND PRINTED BY ST PAUL'S PRESS LTD, MALTA

Contents

Acknowledgements

The author and publishers gratefully acknowledge permission granted by the following copyright owners to quote from their works:

The Bodley Head Ltd. for *A Veld Eclogue: The Pioneers* from *Adamastor* by Roy Campbell; Jonathan Cape Ltd. and Messrs. Holt, Rinehart and Winston Inc. for *Look not in My Eyes for Fear* from *Collected Poems* by A. E. Housman; Constable and Co. Ltd for Translation of Alcuin's *Contention of Spring and Winter* from *Mediaeval Latin Lyrics* by Helen Waddell; Mr. G. S. Fraser for translation of part of *Theocritus's Third Idyll* by himself; Macmillan and Co. Ltd. and The Macmillan Company for *The Resurrection, The Song of the Happy Shepherd, Shepherd and Goatherd, The Man and the Echo* from the *Collected Poems* of W. B. Yeats; Messrs. Faber and Faber Ltd. and New Directions Publishing Corpn. for *An Idyll for Glaucus* from *Selected Poems* of Ezra Pound; Messrs. Faber and Faber and Oxford University Press New York for *An Eclogue for Christmas* from *Collected Poems* by Louis MacNeice; Faber and Faber and October House Inc. for *Goodman Jacksin and the Angel* from *Collected Poems* by George Barker; Messrs. Faber and Faber for *A Young Man's Song* from *Mountains Beneath the Horizon* by William Bell.

The Origins of the Form

The feeling for natural beauty and for the life of the country-side is so universal in poetry, in all ages and in all places, that we are apt to take it for granted. In the following pages however, we shall be concerned with this in a special way. We shall be dealing with a particular poetical convention, which had a definite historical origin in the work of certain Greek poets of the second century before Christ. This began a tradition which was to continue through the classical Latin poets and their successors of the Middle Ages; and which was revived at the Renaissance and has continued down to modern times.

The father of pastoral poetry is **Theocritus** (*c.* 316–*c.* 260 B.C.). This poet was a native of Syracuse in Sicily. Sicily and Southern Italy had for some centuries been settled by Greek colonists, and were to become known, indeed, as Magna Graecia, or Greater Greece. Those Greeks who occupied Sicily had come originally from Arcadia in Southern Greece, and spoke the Doric dialect of that region. Theocritus employed the same dialect in his poems, and the words Doric and Arcadian were henceforth always to be associated with the world of pastoral simplicity which he depicted in his poems. From ancient times, indeed, the Arcadians had been known as the most primitive of the peoples of Greece, and they claimed to be the most ancient – holding that they remembered a time before the moon was created. Their neighbours noted the simplicity of their manners, and also one might add, sometimes their savagery. Lycaon, who drew upon himself the wrath of Zeus by offering him human sacrifice, was an Arcadian hero, and there is evidence that the same savage practice persisted among Arcadian peasants in historical times. Pan, the shaggy goat-footed and goat-horned god, was primarily an Arcadian deity. He might inspire travellers in lonely places with irrational 'panic' terror, and the shepherds feared to pipe at noon lest they should disturb his siesta. Yet, in thoroughly primitive fashion, hunters would flog his statue if he did not grant them success in the chase.

Theocritus's poetry, however, was written not for his countrymen, the Arcadians of Sicily, but for the Greeks of the highly sophisticated and urbanized city of Alexandria. This city, founded by Alexander the Great, was ruled by the dynasty of the Ptolemys. Descendants of one of Alexander's

Macedonian generals, they had become cosmopolitanized and oriental-ized — even to the extent of following the custom of the native Egyptian Pharaohs in marrying their sisters and in inviting their subjects to treat them as divine. But they were also great patrons of learning, of the sciences, art and literature. It was this patronage which attracted Theocritus in common with many other poets of the Greek-speaking world to live and work in the Egyptian city. Alexandria, with its varied population of native Egyptians, Greeks, Jews, and many others, was a cosmopolitan urban centre more like the cities of the modern world than the little city-republics of classical Greece had been. It was and still is a great trading port in which men's lives were not organically related to the life of the surrounding country-side as they had been in those earlier cities. Hence there grew up, as perhaps never before in history, a nostalgia for the life of the country and a tendency to idealize it. It was to the taste thus en-gendered that the pastoral poetry of Theocritus appealed.

The Hellenistic poetry of Alexandria was sophisticated, elegant, scholar-ly, and sometimes sentimental. The poets delighted in the ingenious rehandling of themes from traditional mythology. The gods no longer commanded genuine religious awe, but the stories that were told about them could be made the subject of decorative and fantastic little pictures. This is what the word idyll, the title given to Theocritus's poems, in fact means. The Pastoral Idylls were also later to be called Eclogues,[1] or Selections.

Some of Theocritus's idylls are in fact short mythological narratives, recounting such stories as the carrying off of Hylas, the youth beloved of Heracles, by the nymphs, or the youthful exploits of Heracles him-self. These Epic idylls, or Epyllia as they are called, are typically Hellen-istic, and provide the model for similar treatments of mythological themes both by the Elizabethan and Victorian poets. This is how Tennyson's *Idylls of the King* acquired their title. But they need not further concern us here. Others give us realistic pictures of contemporary life not neces-sarily pastoral. Thus the very lively fifteenth Idyll shows us a party of Sicilian women in Alexandria watching the celebrations of the resurrection of Adonis. It is dramatic in character and is probably influenced by the mimes of Sophron.[2]

---

[1] This word is sometimes spelt Eglogues or Aeglogues by English writers of the sixteenth century. This spelling owes its origin to the belief that the word was derived from the Greek *aix* – a goat, and meant goatherds' songs.

[2] The Greek mimes, of which some of those of another writer, Herondas, have survived, were short dramatic sketches of contemporary life.

We shall see, however, that English poets of the eighteenth century were also to use the form of the dramatic idyll for scenes of contemporary urban life. Theocritus's second idyll depicts Simaetha, a town girl who has been deserted by her lover, attempting to win back his affections by the practice of magical spells. This very vivid and interesting poem was to be imitated by Virgil in a pastoral setting, and the theme of sorcery thus passed into the Pastoral tradition.

It is however Theocritus's pastoral or bucolic[3] poems which represent his most original and characteristic contribution, and with which we are chiefly concerned.

These are scenes from the lives of the shepherds, goatherds, neatherds, farmers and fishermen of Sicily and Southern Italy. They may be considered as in the main realistic pictures of that life. They are idealized only in so far as the harsher aspects are omitted. These shepherds are for the most part free peasants, who own their own flocks and obviously enjoy a reasonable if simple standard of living. This way of life was in fact passing in Theocritus's own generation, and the shepherds of Sicily were being reduced to the status of serfs employed on the estates of large-scale landlords. It is this perhaps which throws its glow of nostalgia over his poetry, as of a lost golden age. But the poems are far removed from that depiction of a wholly idealized and artificial world of refined poetical shepherds into which pastoral poetry was to evolve in later ages.

Theocritus's pastorals are generally dramatic in form, like the mime-poems already noted, consisting of dialogues or monologues. He represents his shepherds as engaged in contests of piping and improvised song, each of the protagonists capping the verses of the other or engaged in what the medieval Scottish poets called a 'flyting', or exchange of mock-serious abuse. This exchange of verses, known as 'amoebean', evidently represents a type of improvised poetry still in use in some parts of Italy. The shepherds also recount the rival charms of their respective objects of affection, or woo girls who are coy and difficult to get. In the latter scenes we may suspect the influence of the more refined and sentimental treatment of love which was becoming fashionable with the Hellenistic poets. There are many references to the local traditions of Sicily. The cyclops Polyphemus, from Homer's Odyssey, whose home commentators had located in Sicily, becomes a sentimental lover wooing the nymph Galatea. Another prominent figure is the shepherd Daphnis, who married a nymph, and who according to Theocritus was slain by Aphrodite for his obstinate fidelity.

---

[3] This word is derived from the Greek *bukolos*, a neatherd.

All nature laments the death of Daphnis. He seems to have been originally a minor vegetation god, who died seasonally with the year, like Attis or Adonis. Here we have the beginnings of the type of Pastoral Elegy, which was to have a long history of literary development.

In Theocritus's first idyll the dying words of Daphnis are thus recounted by the shepherd Thyrsis for the benefit of his friend the Goatherd, who offers him a pipe and a cup as a prize for his singing. The translation is that of C. S. Calverley (1831–84):

> 'Come, king of song, o'er this my pipe, compact
> With wax and honey-breathing, arch thy lip:
> For surely I am torn from life by Love.
>   Forget, sweet Maids, forget your woodland song.
> From thicket now and thorn let violets spring,
> Now let white lilies drape the juniper,
> And pines grow figs, and nature all go wrong:
> For Daphnis dies. Let deer pursue the hounds,
> And mountain-owls outsing the nightingale.
>   Forget, sweet Maids, forget your woodland song.'
>
> So spake he, and he never spake again.
> Fain Aphrodite would have raised his head;
> But all his thread was spun. So down the stream
> Went Daphnis: closed the waters o'er his head
> Dear to the Nine, of nymphs not unbeloved.
>   Now give me goat and cup; that I may milk
> The one, and pour the other to the Muse.
> Fare ye well, Muses, o'er and o'er farewell!
> I'll sing strains lovelier yet in days to be.

As an example of Theocritus's treatment of the theme of love we will quote part of the third idyll in a version by the contemporary poet G. S. Fraser:

> I am off to serenade Amaryllis, and my goats
> Are cropping the high grass, Tityrus is minding them;
> Tityrus, be a good fellow, let the goats graze,
> Then drive them to the springs. Tityrus; but the he-goat,
> The big buff Libyan, careful, or he'll butt you!
>
> Sweet Amaryllis, why do you not await me,
> Looking from your cave to call me? Do you hate me?
> Or when you look at me close, is my nose so squat,
> And bristly my beard? I shall hang myself, that's what!

But look, here are ten apples, I found a store
Just where you said, and tomorrow shall bring more.

O, do look out! Heartsick, I wish I were the bee
That, blundering, buzzes its way into your cave
Past the ivy, the fern that hide you from me!

Who Love is, now I know, harsh god, by sorrow:
Suckled by a lioness, bred in a forest shade:
His fire, once kindled, burns me to the marrow.

O bright and stony glancer from brows of night,
But once, to kiss me, come once to your goatherd's arms:
For even mere vain kisses hold delight.

You will make me tear my garland all to shreds —
The ivy-crown I wear for you, cruel lady,
Where rose-leaves twine with savoury parsley-threads.

(Alas, but what'll befall me? You do not listen at all.)

I will shed my shaggy jerkin and plunge beneath
The waves where the fishermen watch for the tunney-shoals;
And, if you want to, plume yourself on my death!

Theocritus's immediate successors are **Bion** (*c.* 100? B.C.) and **Moschus** (fl. *c.* 150 B.C.). Several pastoral poems by Bion are extant, in which he follows Theocritus's manner closely. But his best known poem is a lament for the dying god, Adonis, probably intended to be sung at a religious festival. He died young, allegedly by poison. Moschus's most important poem is his lament for Bion. In this he developed the Pastoral Elegy a stage further, by picturing the deceased poet as himself a shepherd, and casting him, as it were, in the role of Daphnis in an idealized pastoral world. The form thus established was to become the standard mode in which one poet mourned the death of another. It was imitated, as we shall see shortly, by Virgil, and in English literature is directly or indirectly the model for Milton's *Lycidas*, Shelley's *Adonais*, and Matthew Arnold's *Thyrsis*. The passage, which we quote in the prose translation of Andrew Lang (1844–1912), in which the rustic deities and the whole of nature are depicted mourning for the dead poet, has perhaps been the most influential on later writers:

Thy sudden doom, O Bion, Apollo himself lamented, and the Satyrs mourned thee, and the Priapi in sable raiment, and the Panes sorrow for thy song, and the fountain fairies in the wood made moan, and their tears turned to rivers of waters. And Echo on the rocks laments that thou art silent, and no more she mimics thy voice.

5

And in sorrow for thy fall the trees cast down their fruit, and all the flowers have faded. From the ewes hath flowed no fair milk, nor honey from the hives, nay, it hath perished for mere sorrow in the wax, for now hath thy honey perished, and no more it behoves men to gather the honey of the bees.

When the Romans sought to create for themselves a national literature they modelled their writings closely on those of their Greek predecessors. Thus **Virgil** (70–19 B.C.) when he wrote his *Aeneid* was self-consciously producing a national epic for Rome, modelled upon Homer. His earliest poetic work, *The Eclogues*, was equally closely modelled upon Theocritus. These Pastorals are one step further removed from the realities of rural life though they do include images derived from Virgil's observation of the contemporary Italian peasantry. Nevertheless they are highly literary and imitative in their inspiration, and represent an ideal rather than an actual world. They are however related to contemporary life in a different sort of way — by allusion, or by a kind of allegory. In Virgil's lifetime rural Italy had been devastated by a series of disastrous civil wars, a power-struggle, from which Octavius the nephew and adopted son of Julius Caesar eventually emerged as the Emperor Augustus. Many had lost their lives or had had their estates confiscated, and much of the land had gone out of cultivation. It was Augustus's policy to encourage resettlement of the land; Virgil's second great poem, the *Georgics*, was written to support this. Virgil himself had forfeited his hereditary estates near Mantua during the civil wars but had had them restored to him at the instance of Maecenas, his patron and Augustus's minister. His first *Eclogue* is a dialogue between Tityrus, who represents the poet himself, and another shepherd, Meliboeus, who had lost his estates. In the poem Virgil is both eulogizing Augustus and expressing his compassion for his less fortunate countrymen. We will quote part of this poem in Dryden's translation:

MELIBOEUS
Beneath the Shade which Beechen Boughs diffuse,
You Tityrus entertain your Silvan Muse:
Round the wide World in Banishment we roam,
Forc'd from our pleasing Fields and Native Home:
While stretch'd at Ease you sing your happy loves:
And Amarillis fills the shady Groves.

TITYRUS
These blessings, Friend, a Deity bestow'd:
For never can I deem him less than God.
The tender Firstlings of my Woolly breed

6

Shall on his Holy altar often bleed.
He gave my Kine to graze the Flow'ry Plain,
And to my Pipe renew'd the Rural Strain.

MELIBOEUS

But we must beg our Bread in Climes unknown,
Beneath the scorching or the freezing Zone.
And some to far *Oaxis* shall be sold;
Or try the *Libyan* heat or *Scythian* cold.
The rest among the *Britons* be confin'd;
A Race of Men from all the World dis-join'd.
O! must the wretched Exiles ever mourn,
Nor after length of rolling Years return?
Are we condemn'd by Fate's unjust Decree,
No more our Houses and our Homes to see?
Or shall we mount again the Rural Throne,
And rule the Country Kingdoms, once our own!
Did we for these Barbarians plant and sow,
On these, on these, our happy Fields bestow?
Good heav'n, what dire Effects from Civil Discord flow!
Now let me graft my Pears, and prune the Vine;
The Fruit is theirs, the Labour only mine.
Farewell, my Pastures, my Paternal Stock,
My fruitful Fields, and my more fruitful Flock!
No more, my Goats, shall I behold you climb
The steepy Cliffs, or crop the flow'ry Thyme!
No more, extended in the Grot below,
Shall see you browzing on the Mountain's brow
The prickly Shrubs; and after on the bare,
Lean down the Deep Abyss, and hang in Air!
No more my Sheep shall sip the Morning Dew;
No more my Song shall please the Rural Crew;
Adieu, my tuneful pipe! and all the world adieu!

Though much of this imagery is drawn from Greek pastoral verse, the tone is rather different. The deep-rooted, almost romantic feeling for the fruitfulness of the soil is fundamentally Latin and Virgilian. So too it must be admitted is the poet's underpinning of the developing cult of the divine Emperor, but he is, by implication, not without his criticisms of the political establishment which he had come to accept. It is this which gives its undercurrent of melancholy to the poem, with its sympathy for the defeated.

We have spoken of an element akin to allegory in Virgil's pastorals. This can be illustrated from his handling of the theme of the death of

Daphnis. Virgil's Daphnis is in fact Julius Caesar, who had been officially deified by the senate after the accession of Augustus. The poem thus ends with an apotheosis — an account of Daphnis's ascent to Heaven. This was to have important implications for the handling of the pastoral elegy form by Christian poets. We cite Dryden's version again:

MENALCAS
Daphnis, the Guest of Heav'n, with wond'ring Eyes,
Views in the Milky Way, the starry Skies:
And far beneath him, from the shining Sphere,
Beholds the moving Clouds, and rolling Year.
For this, with cheerful Cries the Woods resound;
The purple Spring arrays the various ground:
The Nymphs and Shepherds dance; and *Pan* himself is Crowned.
The Wolf no longer prowls for nightly Spoils,
Nor Birds the Springes fear, nor Stags the Toils:
For *Daphnis* reigns above; and deals from thence
His Mother's milder Beams, and peaceful Influence.

The concluding line is explained by the fact that the Julian house claimed descent from the goddess Venus.

Virgil's tenth eclogue is also elegiac in tone, and imitates Moschus's lament for Bion. It is dedicated to his patron and fellow-poet Gallus, but celebrates not the latter's death, but his grief at being forsaken by his mistress, Cytheris, poetically called Lycoris. We quote a fragmentary translation of part of this poem, by Shelley:

Melodious Arethusa, o'er my verse
  Shed thou once more the spirit of thy stream:
    .   .   .   .

Who denies verse to Gallus? So, when thou
  Glidest beneath the green and purple gleam
Of Syracusan waters, mayest thou flow
  Unmingled with the bitter Dorian dew!
Begin, and whilst the goats are browsing now
  The soft leaves, in our song let us pursue
The melancholy loves of Gallus. List!
  We sing not to the deaf: the wild woods knew
His sufferings, and their echoes answer....
  Young Naiades, in what far woodlands wild
Wandered ye, when unworthy love possessed
  Our Gallus? Nor where Pindus is up-piled,
Nor where Parnassus' sacred mount, nor where
  Aonian Aganippe spreads its [streams]
    .   .   .   .

The laurels and the myrtle-copses dim,
    The pine-encircled mountain, Maenalus,
The cold crags of Lycaeus weep for him.

.   .   .   .

'What madness is this, Gallus? thy heart's care,
    Lycoris, mid rude camps and Alpine snow,
With willing step pursues another there'.

.   .   .   .

And Sylvan, crowned with rustic coronals,
Came shaking in his speed the budding wands
And heavy lilies which he bore: we knew
Pan the Arcadian [crimsoned-vermilion]
        ... and [he] said,
'Wilt thou not ever cease? Love cares not.
The meadows with fresh streams, the bees with thyme,
The goats with the green leaves of budding spring
Are satiated not – nor Love with tears.'

Virgil introduced into some of his eclogues, themes of a philosophical and religious nature. Thus in the sixth eclogue he makes the wise old satyr, Silenus, give an account of the creation of the world in terms of the Epicurean philosophy, which had already been expounded by Lucretius in his great poem *De Rerum Natura*. But the most striking and original of all Virgil's eclogues is the fourth, the so-called Messianic eclogue. This poem prophesies the coming again of the Golden Age, which is to be ushered in by the birth of a mysterious child. The purpose and origin of this poem have given rise to much speculation. It is addressed to the consul Pollio, apparently on the occasion of the expected birth of his son. But the enormous importance which is attached to this event suggests that it was originally written for some occasion of more universal significance. Virgil's sympathies, during the struggle preceding the accession of Augustus, seem to have been with the party of Mark Antony. An interesting suggestion has been made that the child whose birth is celebrated in the poem was originally Alexander Helios, Antony's son by Cleopatra. Antony and Cleopatra encouraged their subjects to treat them as gods manifest on earth. Antony identified himself with Bacchus (who was regarded as the same as the Egyptian god Osiris), while Cleopatra assumed the person of the goddess Isis; their children they called Helios, the Sun, and Selene, the Moon. In so doing they were following the traditions of the oriental peoples whom they ruled. The imagery of the poem may thus reflect the prophetic and religious aspirations of these peoples, which Antony and Cleopatra sought to exploit. In the Middle Ages the fourth eclogue was taken to be a prophecy of the coming birth of Christ, and Virgil was 'the prophet of the gentiles'. Even as late as our own Augustan age, Dryden and Pope still accept this view of the poem. The idea is not perhaps so far-fetched. The eschatological expectations of the peoples of the Near-East formed part of the milieu in which Christianity developed — a *preparatio evangelii*. Those who accept Christ's birth as a divinely ordained event may well see the Spirit as working in Virgil's poem also.

We quote part of the poem in Calverley's translation:

> Come are those last days that the Sybil sang:
> The ages' mighty march begins anew.
> Now comes the virgin, Saturn reigns again:
> Now from high heaven descends a wondrous race.
> Thou on the newborn babe — who first shall end
> That age of iron, bid a golden dawn
> Upon the broad world
>
> .   .   .   .
>
> On thee, child, everywhere shall earth, untilled,
> Show'r, her first baby-offerings, vagrant stems
> Of ivy, foxglove, and gay briar, and bean;
> Unbid the goats shall come big-uddered home,
> Nor monstrous lions scare the herded kine.
> Thy cradle shall be full of pretty flowers:
> Die must the serpent, treacherous poison-plants
> Must die; and Syria's roses spring like weeds.
> But, soon as thou canst read of hero-deeds
> Such as thy father wrought, and understand
> What is true worth: the champaign day by day
> Shall grow more yellow with the waving corn;
> From the wild bramble purpling then shall hang
> The grape; and stubborn oaks drop honeydew.
> Yet traces of that guile of elder days
> Shall linger; bidding men tempt seas in ships,
> Gird towns with walls, cleave furrows in the land.
> Then a new Typhis shall arise, to man
> New argosies with heroes: then shall be
> New wars; and once more shall be bound for Troy,
> A mightier Achilles.
>
>   After this,
> When thou hast grown and strengthened into man,
> The pilot's self shall range the seas no more;
> Nor, each land teeming with the wealth of all,
> The floating pines exchange their merchandise.

> Vines shall not need the pruning-hook, nor earth
> The harrow: ploughmen shall unyoke their steers.

The reign of Saturn, before he was deposed by his son Jupiter, was supposed to have coincided with the Golden Age. At its close Astraea, the goddess of justice, left the earth and became the constellation of the Virgin. This word was of course taken by medieval readers to refer to the Virgin Mary. Typhis was the helmsman of the Argo.

The fourth eclogue has inspired poets other than Christians who held a prophetic view of human history. Thus Shelley echoes this poem in the concluding chorus of his drama *Hellas*:

> The world's great age begins anew,
>   The golden years return,
> The earth doth like a snake renew
>   Her winter weeds outworn:
> Heaven smiles, and faiths and empires gleam
> Like wrecks of a dissolving dream.
>
> A brighter Hellas rears its mountains
>   From waves serener far;
> A new Peneus rolls his fountains
>   Against the morning star.
> Where fairer Tempes bloom, there sleep
> Young Cyclads on a sunnier deep.
>
> A loftier Argo cleaves the main,
>   Fraught with a later prize;
> Another Orpheus sings again,
>   And loves, and weeps, and dies.
> A new Ulysses leaves once more
> Calypso for his native shore.
>
> .   .   .   .
>
> Saturn and Love their long repose
>   Shall burst, more bright and good
> Than all who fell, than One who rose,
>   Than many unsubdued:
> Not gold, not blood, their altar dowers,
> But votive tears and symbol flowers.

Yeats draws on the same stock of imagery, though in a different way, in one of the songs in his play *The Resurrection*:

> I saw a staring virgin stand
> Where holy Dionysus died,

And tear the heart out of his side,
And lay the heart upon her hand
And bear that beating heart away;
And then did all the Muses sing
Of Magnus Annus at the spring,
As though God's death were but a play.

Another Troy must rise and set,
Another lineage feed the crow,
Another Argo's painted prow
Drive to a flashier bauble yet.
The Roman Empire stood appalled:
It dropped the reins of peace and war
When that fierce virgin and her Star
Out of the fabulous darkness called.

We must now notice a prose work of late antiquity – the Greek pastoral romance *Daphnis and Chloe*, by **Longus**, who is believed to have lived some time between the beginning of the third and the end of the fifth century A.D. This work formed the principal model for the Pastoral Romance which was developed as an important form by the writers of the Renaissance period. The story is set in the island of Lesbos, but we are now in a completely idealized and sentimentalized pastoral world with very little relation to historical reality. Daphnis and Chloe are boy and girl lovers whose story is rendered interesting by various exciting events, such as a raid by pirates, and who eventually turn out to be the long-lost children of rich parents. But the main theme is the education of Daphnis, who although passionately in love with Chloe is totally, and most improbably for a shepherd, ignorant of certain essential biological facts. This is however a work of very great charm, as the following passage from the translation of George Thornley (b. 1614), may show:

It was the beginning of Spring, and all the flowers of the Launs, Meadowes, Valleyes, and Hills, were now blowing; all was fresh, and green, and odorous. The Bee's humming from the flowers, the Bird's warbling from the groves, the Lamb's skipping on the hills, were pleasant to the ear, and eye. And now when such a fragrancy had filled those blest and happy fields, both the old men and the young, would imitate the pleasant things they heard, and saw; and hearing how the Birds did chant it, they began to carroll too; and seeing how the Lambs skipt, tript their light and nimble measures; then to emulate the Bees, they fall to cull the fairest flowers. Some of which in toysome sport they cast in one another's bosoms, and of some plaited garlands for the Nymphs. And always keeping near together, had, and did all things in common: for Daphnis often gathered the straggling sheep; and Chloe often drove the bolder ventrous Goats from the crags, and precipices; and sometimes to one of them, the care of both the flocks was left, while the other did intend some pretty knack, or Toysome play. For all their sport, were sports of children, and of shepherds. Chloe scudding up and down, and here and there picking up the windlestraws; would make in plats, a Trap to catch a Grasshopper; and be so wholly bent on that, that she was care-lesse of her flocks. Daphnis on the other side, having cut the slender reeds, and bored the quils, or intervals between the joynts, and with his soft wax joyned and fitted one to the other; took no care but to practise, or devise some tune, even from morning, to the twilight.

Principally owing to the continuing prestige of Virgil, the eclogue form was not infrequently employed by the Latin poets of the Middle Ages. But their poems, the work of monks and scholars, have little of the fresh feeling for nature characteristic of ancient pastoral poetry. As an example, we may cite in Helen Waddell's translation, a poem by an Englishman, the great scholar **Alcuin** (735–804) of York, who worked in the atmosphere of the reawakening humanism of Charlemagne's court:

> From the high mountains the shepherds came together,
> Gathered in the spring light under branching trees,
> Came to sing songs, Daphnis, old Palemon,
> All making ready to sing the cuckoo's praises.
> Thither came Spring, girdled with a garland,
> Thither came Winter, with his shaggy hair.
> Great strife between them on the cuckoo's singing.

Spring. I would that he were here,
> Cuckoo!
> Of all winged things most dear,
> To every roof the most beloved guest.
> Bright-billed, good songs he sings.

Winter. Let him not come,
> Cuckoo!
> Stay on in the dark cavern where he sleeps,
> For Hunger is the company he brings.

Spring. I would that he were here!
> Cuckoo!
> Gay buds come with him, and the frost is gone,
> Cuckoo, the age-long comrade of the sun.
> The days are longer and the light serene.

Winter. Let him not come,
> Cuckoo!

For toil comes with him and he wakens wars,
Breaks blessed quiet and disturbs the world,
And sea and earth alike sets travailing.

Spring. And what are you that throw your blame on him?
That huddle sluggish in your half-lit caves
After your feasts of Venus, bouts of Bacchus?

Winter. Riches are mine and joy of revelling,
And sweet is sleep, the fire on the hearth stone.
Nothing of these he knows, and does his treasons.

Spring. Nay, but he brings the flowers in his bright bill,
And he brings honey, nests are built for him.
The sea is quiet for his journeying,
Young ones begotten, and the fields are green.

Winter. I like not these things which are joy to you.
I like to count the gold heaped in my chests;
And feast, and then to sleep, and then to sleep.

Spring. And who, thou slug-abed, got thee thy wealth?
And who would pile thee any wealth at all,
If spring and summer did not toil for thee?

Winter. Thou speakest truth; indeed they toil for me.
They are my slaves, and under my dominion.
As servants for their lord, they sweat for me.

Spring. No lord, but poor and beggarly and proud.
Thou couldst not feed thyself a single day
But for his charity who comes, who comes!
　　　　　Cuckoo!

Then old Palemon spake from his high seat,
And Daphnis, and the crowd of faithful shepherds.
'Have done, have done, Winter, spendthrift and foul,
And let the shepherd's friend, the cuckoo, come.
And may the happy buds break on our hills,
Green be our grazing, peace in the ploughed fields,
Green branches give their shadow to tired men,
The goats come to the milking, udders full,
The birds call to the sun, each one his note.
Wherefore, O cuckoo, come, O cuckoo, come!
For thou art Love himself, the dearest guest,
And all things wait thee, sea and earth and sky.
All hail, beloved: through all ages, hail!'

This picture of Spring belongs to Northern Europe in the Dark Ages. Men have to labour at the spring sowing and ploughing, but go hungry because of the Lenten fast, and because their reserve stocks of grain and salt meat are used up. There is also danger from Danish pirates at their spring raiding. The poem is an early example of the medieval form known as the *débat*. This seems to have developed out of the Eclogue form, from those classical poems in which, as we have seen, the shepherds engage in singing contests or discuss the rival charms of their loves. In the medieval poems the speakers may be human, or they may be (as here) allegorical personifications, or beasts, or, very frequently, birds. These stand for and argue opposed points of view. The most important English examples include the thirteenth-century *The Owl and the Nightingale*, the fifteenth-century *The Cuckoo and the Nightingale* (once attributed to Chaucer, but now known to be by Sir Thomas Clanvowe), and William Dunbar's *The Two Mariit Wemen and the Wedo*.

The name 'pastorals' may also be applied in the later Middle Ages, in France and England, to popular poems of a dramatic character, associated with the Whitsuntide and Mayday games.[4] The principal characters are Robin (in England, Robin Hood), and his girl friend Marion, as in the well known musical play by the French troubadour **Adam de la Hale** (1238–88). It is with these, rather than with the classical tradition, that the *Robene and Makyne* of the Scottish poet **Robert Henryson** (1430?–1506), which has been called our first pastoral, is to be connected.

It is true that this Robene is a shepherd 'Keepand a flock of fe'. He is wooed by Makyne, but coolly rejects her advances:

> 'Robene, thou reivis my roif and rest;
> I luve bot thee alane.'
> 'Makyne, adieu, the sun gois west,
> The day, is near hand gane.'
> 'Robene, in dule I am so drest,
> That luve will be my bane,'
> 'Ga luve, Makyne, wherever thou list,
> For leman I lo'e nane.'

Robene goes home, leaving Makyne disconsolate. But subsequently

---

[4] There is also the *pastourelle*. This is a Romance lyric form, consisting of a dialogue between a knight and a shepherdess whom he seeks to seduce. An English example is "'Hey, troly loly lo, maid, whither go you?'" No. XXVIII in Chambers and Sidgwick's *Early English Lyrics*. The form has survived in folk-song: e.g. 'Where are you going, my pretty maid?'

the tables are turned. It is now he how woos, and Makyne who replies:

> 'Robene, thou has heard sung and say,
> In gestis and storeis auld,
> The man that will nocht when he may
> Sall have nocht when he wald.
> I pray to Jesu every day
> Mot eke their carës cauld,
> That first presses with thee to play,
> Be firth, forest, or fauld.'

The beginnings of the Renaissance in fourtheenth- and fifteenth-century Italy led to a revival of interest in the eclogue form. **Petrarch** (1304–74) and **Boccaccio** (1313?–75) both wrote Latin poems in this form, but more important for their subsequent influence were the Latin Pastorals of **Mantuan** (1448–1516), a Carmelite monk whose real name was Johannes Baptista Spagnola. These had a European vogue and were used as school texts in England in Elizabethan times. He was one of the favourite poets of Holofernes, the pedantic schoolmaster in Shakespeare's *Love's Labour's Lost*. We have already noticed an element akin to allegory in some of Virgil's eclogues. This is extended and adapted to a specific Christian purpose by both Petrarch and Mantuan. The language of both the Old and the New Testaments continually makes use of pastoral imagery to express God's relationship to his people. Christ spoke of himself as the Good Shepherd, and a Christian minister is a Pastor, whose devotion to his flock is contrasted with that of the Hireling. Petrarch and Mantuan unite these metaphors with the traditional language of Pastoral, and it was natural for them to do so in an age when ecclesiastical institutions were becoming the subject of increasing criticism, and often of caustic satire. **Alexander Barclay** (1475?–1552) was the first to adopt this mode in English verse. Probably of Scottish origin, he wrote his eclogues when a monk at Ely. Of his five eclogues the last two are translations of two of Mantuan's, while the first three are adapted from another Humanist work, the *Miseriae Curialium* of Aeneas Sylvius, afterwards Pope Pius II (1405–64). This work is a satire, contrasting the corruption of courts with the simplicity of rural life. This forms a main theme in Barclay's eclogues, and was to be continued by his Elizabethan successors.

It must be confessed that Barclay, though worthy, is a dull poet. Nevertheless he does occasionally succeed in introducing a touch of genuinely English local colour:

Amintas was formall and proper in his geare,
A man on his cloke should not espye a heare,
Nor of his clothing one wrinkle stande a wry,
In London he learned to go so manerly,
High on his bonet stacke a fayre brouche of tinne,
His purses lining was simple, poore and thinne:
But a lordes stomake and a beggers pouche
Full ill accordeth, suche was this comely slouch,
In the towne and citie so longe ietted had he
That from thence he fled for det and pouertie,
No wafrer, tauerne, alehouse or tauerner,
To him was there hid while he was hosteler,
First was he hosteler, and then a wafrer,
Then a costermonger, and last a tauerner,
About all London there was no proper prim
But long time had bene familier with him,
But when coyne fayled no fauour more had he,
Wherfore he was glad out of the towne to flee.
But shepheard Faustus was yet more fortunate,
For alway was he content with his estate,
Yet nothing he had to comfort him in age,
Saue a milch cowe and a poore cotage,
The towne he used, and great pleasour he had
To see the citie oft time while he was lad.
For milke and butter he hither brought to sell,
But never thought he in citie for to dwell,
For well he noted the mad enormitie,
Enuy, fraude, malice and suche iniquitie
Which reigne in cities, therefore he led his life
Uplande in village without debate and strife.

Barclay is an interesting link between the Middle Ages and the Renaissance. His other works include a translation of the Roman historian Sallust, and of *Das Narrenschiff* (The Ship of Fools), a satire by the German, Sebastian Brant. But his poetic style is purely medieval. It is modelled on that of Lydgate, but his language is simpler and more colloquial. His work is mainly of historical interest, and does not seem to have influenced his successors. Parallels between his eclogues and those of Googe and Spenser have been shown to be due to the later poets' drawing independently on the same passages in Mantuan. Nevertheless in these eclogues he planted a seed which was to burgeon luxuriantly in the coming centuries.

2

The Elizabethans

In the Elizabethan age the pastoral mode becomes a dominant form. Its imagery is found not only in the formal eclogue but also in the lyric, the drama, narrative verse and prose fiction. However, the earliest of the Elizabethan pastoralists, **Barnaby Googe** (1504–94), gives few hints of the vitality which was to come. His *Eglogs* (1563) do not really show any advance on Barclay's. Indeed, his monotonous fourteeners are less alive than Barclay's irregular Lydgatian five-stress lines. Like Barclay he imitates and translates Mantuan, and uses the pastoral as a vehicle for Christian allegory and ecclesiastical satire. He is a strong Protestant, and the following passage describes with some passion the persecutions under Queen Mary I. Coridon is evidently Bishop Bonner, Daphnes is Cranmer, and Alexis is Latimer or Ridley:

> This *Coridon* come from the Carte,
>   In honour chiefe doth sytte,
> And governes us: because he hath
>   a Crabbed, Clownish wytte.
> Now se the Churlysh Crueltye,
>   that in hys harte remayns.
> The selye sheape that Shephards good,
>   have fosterd up wyth Paynes,
> And browght awaye, from Stynkyng dales
>   on pleasant Hylles to feade:
> O Cruell Clownish Coridon
>   O cursed Carlish Seade:
> The simple Shepe, constrayned he,
>   theyr Pasture swete to leave,
> And to theyr old corrupted Grasse,
>   enforceth them to cleave.
> Such Shepe, as would not them obaye
>   but in theyr Pasture byde,
> With (cruell flames,) they did consume
>   and vex on every syde.
> And with the shepe, the Shephardes good,
>   (O hatefull Hounds of Hell,)

> They did torment, and dryve them out,
>> in Places farre to dwell.
> There dyed *Daphnes* for his Shepe,
>> the chiefest of them all.
> And fayre *Alexis* flamde in Fyre,
>> who never perysshe shall.
> O Shephards wayle, for *Daphnes* deth,
>> *Alexis* hap lament,
> And curs the force and cruell hartes,
>> that them to death have sent.

Something of the new poetic spirit does breathe in Googe's verse when he treats of love. Here he can achieve a certain lyricism:

> Doste thou entende agayne, to sewe
>> for mercye at her handes?
> As soone thou mayst go plow ye rocks,
>> and reape upon the Sandes.
> Draw nere O mighty Herd of beasts
>> syth no man els is bye,
> Your Herdman longe that hathe you kept,
>> *Dametas* now must dye.

Googe's verse may seem pedestrian, but it is no worse than most of that which appeared during the early years of Elizabeth's reign, and considerably better than some. We should bear this in mind in order to realize the impact which **Spenser** (1552?–99) made when in 1579 *The Shepheard's Calender* appeared. Here, all at once, we find an excitement of language, and an astonishing metrical virtuosity, which signalized that for the first time for nearly two centuries a truly great poet was writing in England. Its importance for English poetry is comparable to the appearance of Wordsworth's and Coleridge's *Lyrical Ballads* in 1798, or of Eliot's *Prufrock* in 1916.

Spenser has read the Greek pastoral poets as well as Virgil and Mantuan. He imitates all of them, and also the French poet **Clément Marot** (1495–1544). Marot had given French rustic names to the speakers in his pastoral poems instead of the traditional Greek ones. Spenser adopts some of these, such as Thenot and Perigot, while to other characters he gives English names such as Willy, Thomalin, Cuddy, Diggon Davy, and so on. He represents himself by Colin Clout (the name is taken from one of Skelton's satires), while Hobbinol is Spenser's Cambridge friend, the pamphleteer and literary theorist, Gabriel Harvey. The story of Colin's love for Rosalind, and Hobbinol's love for him, runs through several of the 'Æglogues' (this is Spenser's spelling of the word), and gives them a dramatic and partly autobiographical unity. In contrast to this is the allegorical and satirical treatment of the religious question in the manner of Mantuan. This begins with the *débat* between Piers and Palinode in the May Æglogue, continues in the July Æglogue (written in fourteeners, but more lively than those of Googe), and the September Æglogue between Hobbinol and Diggon Davy. In all of these the tone is strongly Protestant.

In the May Æglogue two elderly shepherds are watching the May Day games. Piers stands for the Protestant point of view, and Palinode for the Catholic. The name Piers is probably taken from Piers Plowman, for Langland's radical criticism of the abuses of his time led to the sixteenth-century reformers treating him as a forerunner. It will be noted that there is a great deal of poetic feeling in Palinode's description of the May games though Spenser's point of view is that of Piers. This division of sensibility is rather typically Spenserian. Spenser follows those antiquaries who believed that the English May Day ceremonies were derived from, or were identical with, the pagan Roman Floralia. Pan here, of course, stands for the Christian God.

> *Palinode.* Sicker this morrow, no longer ago,
> I saw a shoal of shepherds outgo
> With singing, and shouting, and jolly cheer:
> Before them rode a lusty tabrere,
> That to the many a horn-pipe played,
> Whereto they dancen, each one with his maid.
> To see those folks make such jouissance,
> Made my heart after the pipe to dance:
> Then to the green wood they speeden hem all,
> To fetchen home May with their musicall:
> And home they bringen in a royal throne,
> Crowned as king: and his queen attone
> Was Lady Flora, on whom did attend
> A fair flock of faeries, and a fresh bend
> Of lovely nymphs. (O that I were there,
> To helpen the ladies their maybush bear!)
> Ah! Piers, bene not thy teeth on edge, to think
> How great sport they gainen with little swink?
>
> *Piers.* Perdie, so far am I from envy,
> That their fondness inly I pity:
> Those faitours little regarden their charge,
> While they, letting their sheep run at large,

Passen their time, that should be sparely spent,
In lustihead and wanton merriment.
Thilke same bene shepherds for the devil's stead,
That playen, while their flocks be unfed:
Well is it seen, their sheep bene not their own,
That letten them run at random alone:
But they bene hired for little pay
Of other, that caren as little as they
What fallen the flock, so they han the fleece,
And get all the gain, paying but a piece.
I muse, what account both these will make
The one for the hire, which he doth take,
And th'other for leaving his lord's task,
When great Pan account of shepherds shall ask.

Each of the twelve poems is set in one of the twelve months of the year; where the subject matter is not obviously related to the time of year of the setting, it seems to me possible that there is an astrological relation.[1]

In the December Æglogue, in which as in the January Æglogue, Colin Clout is the sole speaker, this scheme is summed up in the symbolism of the four seasons and the four ages of man. Thus Spring is related to childhood:[2]

'Whilom in youth, when flowered my joyful spring,
Like swallow swift I wand'red here and there;
For heat of heedless lust me so did sting,
That I of doubted danger had no fear:
I went the wasteful woods and forest wide,
Withouten dread of wolves to bene espied.

[1] This is explicit in the July and November Æglogues, though in the latter, Spenser is curiously in error in supposing the sun to enter Pisces in that month; it should be Sagittarius. In the May Æglogue the May Day games are the starting point for the *debât* between Piers and Palinode; but Piers's fable of the Fox and the Kid is a story of theft and trickery appropiate to Mercury, the ruler of the May sign of Gemini. In the June Æglogue Colin's passion for Rosalind is subdued by the lunar and watery influences of the sign of Cancer. Mars is the ruler of Aries (March) and Scorpio (November); in the March Æglogue we find Cupid, the son of Mars and Venus, in arms, while the November Æglogue is devoted to the Martial theme of epic poetry. For the possible astrological framework of the *Faerie Queene* see Alistair Fowler, *Spenser and the Numbers of Time*.
[2] The tone of this is almost Wordsworthian. It may be a coincidence that the robbing of the raven's nest and of the nut tree are significant incidents in the corresponding section of *The Prelude*; but it seems to me at least possible that Wordsworth had this æglogue of Spenser at the back of his mind when planning his poem.

I wont to range amid the mazy thicket,
And gather nuts to make me Christmas game,
And joyéd oft to chase the trembling pricket,
Or hunt the heartless hare till she were tame.
    What reckéd I of wintry age's waste? —
    Then deeméd I my spring would ever last.

How often have I scaled the craggy oak,
All to dislodge the raven of her nest?
How have I weariéd with many a stroke
The stately walnut-tree, the while the rest
    Under the tree fell all for nuts at strife?
    For ylike to me was liberty and life.

And for I was in thilk same looser years,
(Whether the Muse so wrought me from my birth,
Or I too much believed my shepherd peers,)
Somedeal ybent to song and music's mirth,
    A good old shepherd, Wrenock was his name,
    Made me by art more cunning in the same.

The language of *The Shepheard's Calender* is peculiar. The vocabulary has Chaucerian elements, but it is not identical with that of *The Faerie Queene*, in which Spenser appears to have used Chaucerian archaism as an equivalent for the archaic epic dialect of the Homeric poems. In *The Shepheard's Calender* he attempts to give the effect of the Doric dialect of Theocritus by introducing a number of words from English rustic dialect — mainly that of Lancashire. Chaucer, the Tityrus of the poems, is however his master:

THENOT
But shall I tell thee a tale of truth,
Which I conned of Tityrus in my youth,
Keeping his sheep on the hills of Kent?

CUDDIE
To nought more, Thenot, my mind is bent
Than to hear novels of his devise;
They bene so well thewed, and so wise,
Whatever that good old man bespake.

THENOT
Many meet tales of youth did he make,
And some of love, and some of chivalry.

In his envoi to the poems Spenser also refers to 'the Pilgrim that the Ploughman played awhile', that is to say to Langland. In the February Æglogue, from which the passage quoted above is taken, and in the satirical May and September Æglogues, the metre is a rough four-stress line in what Gerard Manley Hopkins was to term 'sprung rhythm'. This is not really Chaucerian but represents Chaucer's verse as Spenser and his contemporaries read it. The significance of the terminal 'e' in Chaucer had been forgotten, and their texts were also often corrupt and defective. But Spenser in the other æglogues employs a great variety of metres. The January and December Æglogues are in the quatrain-and-couplet stanza later to be used by Shakespeare for *Venus and Adonis*. But Spenser departs from tradition in also introducing elaborate lyrical forms into the pastoral. Thus the Theocritean singing-match in the August Æglogue becomes a real game of rhyme-capping, reminiscent of English folk-song. But it is followed by a sestina, a modified version of a highly sophisticated form for which Spenser had Italian models. One of the best known and most successful of Spenser's lyrics is the Song to Elisa from the April Æglogue:

> Ye dainty nymphs, that in this blessed brook
> > Do bathe your breast,
> Forsake your wat'ry bowers, and hither look,
> > At my request:
> And eke you virgins, that on Parnasse dwell,
> Whence floweth Helicon, the learned well,
> > Help me to blaze
> > Her worthy praise,
> Which in her sex doth all excel.
>
> Of fair Elisa be your silver song,
> > That blessed wight:
> The flower of virgins, may she flourish long,
> > In princely plight.
> For she is Syrinx' daughter, without spot,
> Which Pan, the shepherds' god, of her begot:
> > So sprong her grace
> > Of heavenly race,
> No mortal blemish may her blot.
>
> See, where she sits upon the grassy green,
> > (O seemly sight)
> Yclad in scarlet, like a maiden queen,
> > And ermines white:
> Upon her head a cremosin coronet,

> With damask roses and daffadillies set:
>> Bay leaves between,
>> And primroses green,
> Embellish the sweet violet.

More ambitious is the lament for Dido from the November Æglogue, written, as Spenser's annotator E. K. tells us, in imitation of Marot's elegy for the queen of King Louis the XII of France. This is a pastoral elegy leading to an apotheosis, which now has a definitely Christian colouring:

> Why wail we then? why weary we the gods with plaints,
> As if some evil were to her betight?
> She reigns a goddess now among the saints,
> That whilom was the saint of shepherds' light,
> And is installéd now in heaven's height.
>> I see thee, blessed soul, I see
>> Walk in Elysian fields so free.
>> O happy herse!
> Might I once come to thee (O that I might!);
>> O joyful verse!

The world of *The Shepheard's Calender* has its own imaginative validity. It is partly the literary idealized world of classical pastoral, partly the real world of contemporary English shepherds, but most of all the inner world of Spenser's imagination. Thus the story of the shepherd boy's encounter with the god of Love in the March Æglogue is modelled on a poem by Bion. It retains the Alexandrian prettiness of its original but also gives it an English and earthy reality:

>> It was upon a holiday,
>> When shepherds' grooms han leave to play,
>>> I cast to go a shooting.
>> Long wand'ring up and down the land,
>> With bow and bolts in either hand,
>>> For birds in bushes tooting,
>> At length within an ivy tod
>> (There shrouded was the little god)
>>> I heard a busy bustling.
>> I bent my bolt against the bush,
>> Listening if any thing did rush,
>>> But then heard no more rustling.
>> Then, peeping close into the thick,
>> Might see the moving of some quick,
>>> Whose shape appearéd not:

But were it faery, fiend, or snake,
My courage yearned it to awake,
  And manfully thereat shot.
With that sprang forth a naked swain
With spotted wings, like peacock's train,
  And laughing lope to a tree;
His gilden quiver at his back,
And silver bow, which was but slack,
  Which lightly he bent at me.
That seeing, I levelléd again
And shot at him with might and main,
  As thick as it had hailed.
So long I shot, that all was spent;
Then pumice stones I hastly hent
  And threw; but nought availed:
He was so wimble and so wight,
From bough to bough he leppéd light,
  And oft the pumice latched.
Therewith affrayed, I ran away;
But he, that erst seemed but to play,
  A shaft in earnest snatched,
And hit me running in the heel:
For then I little smart did feel,
  But soon it sore increaséd;
And now it rankleth more and more,
And inwardly it fest'reth sore,
  Ne wot I how to cease it.

This union of the ideal and the actual is characteristically Spenserian.
  Spenser had not done with the pastoral convention when he completed
The Shepheard's Calender. He employs it in the partly autobiographical
Colin Clout's Come Home Again, and in two elegies, *Daphnaida* (on the
death of Douglas Howard, wife of the courtier and minor poet, Arthur
Gorges) and *Astrophel* (on the death of Sir Philip Sidney, to whom *The
Shepheard's Calender* had been dedicated). *Daphnaida* is really in the form
of a medieval allegorical *complaint*, descending from Chaucer's *Boke of the
Duchesse* and the pseudo-Chaucerian *Complaint of the Black Knight*
(probably by Lydgate). But this convention is counterpointed, as it were,
against typical pastoral imagery:

How happy was I, when I saw her lead
The shepherd's daughters dancing in a round!
How trimly would she trace and softly tread

The tender grass, with rosy garland crowned!
And when she list advance her heavenly voice,
Both nymphs and muses nigh she made astound,
And flocks and shepherds caused to rejoice.

But now, ye shepherd lasses, who shall lead
Your wand'ring troops, or sing your virelays?
Or who shall dight your bowers, sith she is dead
That was the lady of your holidays:
Let now your bliss be turnéd into bale,
And into plaints convert your joyous plays,
And with the same fill every hill and dale.

Astrophel follows more closely the form of the classical pastoral elegy.
It owes something to Bion's lament for Adonis, as well as to Moschus and
Virgil. The death of the hero is pictured, like that of Adonis, as due to a
fatal encounter with a wild beast, thus allegorizing Sidney's actual death
at the battle of Zutphen. The poem concludes with a formal complaint,
The Doleful Lay of Clorinda (supposed to be written by Sidney's sister,
the Countess of Pembroke). This includes a Christian apotheosis, in which
the soul of Sidney is represented as reborn as an infant in Paradise:

Ah! no: it is not dead, ne can it die,
But lives for aye, in blissful Paradise:
Where like a new-born babe it soft doth lie,
In bed of lilies wrapt in tender wise;
And compassed all about with roses sweet,
And dainty violets from head to feet.

There thousand birds, all of celestial brood,
To him do sweetly carol day and night;
And with strange notes, of him well understood,
Lull him asleep in angelic delight;
Whilst in sweet dream to him presented be
Immortal beauties, which no eye may see.

Sidney has also generally been identified with Sir Calidore, the hero
of the sixth book of the *Faerie Queene*, the *Legend of Courtesy*. There is
no need to quarrel with this tradition: Sidney certainly exemplified that
virtue. After the austere and rather unrewarding fifth book, the *Legend of
Justice*, Spenser seems to turn with a kind of relief, which many of his
readers have shared, to the idyllic world of the sixth. Perhaps the most
famous passage is that in Canto X in which Calidore comes upon Colin
Clout, piping to the naked Graces and his Rosalind:

She was, to weete, that jolly Shepheard's lasse,
Which piped there unto that merry rout;
That jolly shepheard, which there piped, was
Poore Colin Clout, (who knows not Colin Clout?)
He pypt apace, whilest they him daunst about.
Pype, jolly shepheard, pype thou now apace
Unto thy love that made thee low to lout:
Thy love is present there with thee in place;
Thy love is there advaunst to be another Grace.

Sir Philip Sidney (1554–86) is also appropriate as the hero of this book of *The Faerie Queene* as himself the author of a pastoral romance. The model for this form, as we have seen, is *Daphnis and Chloe*. But it was given a European vogue in the Renaissance by the *Diana* of the Spanish writer **Jorge Montemayor** (1520?–61), and it is this work which Sidney imitates. *The Countess of Pembroke's Arcadia*, so called because Sidney first wrote it for the entertainment of his sister, is one of the great works of Elizabethan literature, comparable in scope and importance to the *Faerie Queene*. It is set in an idealized ancient Greek Arcadia, thus described in an often quoted passage:

There were hilles which garnished their proud heights with stately trees: humble valleis, whose base estate semed comforted with refreshing of silver rivers: meadows, enameld with al sorts of ey-pleasing floures: thickets, which being lined with most pleasant shade, were witnessed so to by the chereful deposition of many wel-tuned birds: each pasture stored with sheep feding with sober security, while the prety lambs with bleting oratory craved the dams comfort: here a shepherds boy piping, as though he should never be old: there a yong shepheard-esse knitting, and withall singing, and it seemed that her voice comforted her hands to work, and her hands kept time to her voices musick. As for the houses of the country. (for many houses came under their eye) they were all scattered, no two being one by th'other, and yet not so far off as that it barred mutual succour: a shew, as it were, of an accompanable solitariness, and of a civil wildness.

But this passage is not so typical of the work as a whole, as it has sometimes been taken to be. As Sidney worked on the *Arcadia* its scope extended from that of a simple pastoral romance to a full-scale prose epic. It contains not only incidents of war, chivalry, and courtly love, but also character-drawing and analysis of considerable complexity and sophistication. Its real importance is perhaps as the principal forerunner in English of the psychological novel. It is no accident that Richardson's Pamela takes her name from one of Sidney's heroines.

But we should not forget the poems with which the elaborately rhetorical prose of the *Arcadia* is interspersed. Many of these reflect the contemporary fashion, of which Gabriel Harvey was a leading publicist, of imitating classical metres. But the *Arcadia* also contains the famous 'My true love hath my heart and I have his' and the elaborate double sestina between Strephon and Cleius. The latter is rather too long to give in full here, and if not so quoted the point of its form would be lost.

Pastoral imagery came to pervade Elizabethan lyrical and madrigal verse to such a degree, that it would be tedious to attempt a survey of that field here. *The Passionate Shepherd to His Love* by **Christopher Marlowe** (1564–93), one of the earliest and best of its kind, may stand here for the type of a whole class:

> Come live with me and be my love,
> And we will all the pleasures prove
> That hills and valleys, dale and field,
> And all the craggy mountains yield.
>
> There will we sit upon the rocks
> And see the shepherds feed their flocks,
> By shallow rivers, to whose falls
> Melodious birds sing madrigals.
>
> There will I make thee beds of roses
> And a thousand fragrant posies,
> A cap of flowers, and a kirtle
> Embroider'd all with leaves of myrtle.
>
> A gown made of the finest wool,
> Which from our pretty lambs we pull,
> Fair linéd slippers for the cold,
> With buckles of the purest gold.
>
> A belt of straw and ivy buds
> With coral clasps and amber studs:
> And if these pleasures may thee move,
> Come live with me and be my love.
>
> .   .   .   .
>
> The shepherd swains shall dance and sing
> For thy delight each May-morning:
> If these delights thy mind may move,
> Then live with me and be my love.

We may note that, beautiful as it is, the imagery is entirely artificial, without any attempt at realism. Shoes with buckles of the purest gold would be an expensive present for a shepherdess, nor would she be likely to eat off silver dishes at an ivory table. And even a Canterbury shoemaker's son might have known that you do not pull wool from lambs, and that it would be cruel to try to do so. The poem in fact elicited a number of replies, of which the best known is that of **Sir Walter Raleigh** (1552?–1618):

> If all the world and love were young,
> And truth in every shepherd's tongue,
> These pretty pleasures might me move
> To live with thee and be thy love.
>
> But time drives flocks from field to fold,
> When rivers rage and rocks grow cold;
> And Philomel becometh dumb;
> The rest complains of cares to come.
>
> The flowers do fade, and wanton fields
> To wayward Winter reckoning yields:
> A honey tongue, a heart of gall,
> Is fancy's spring, but sorrow's fall.
>
> Thy gowns, thy shoes, thy beds of roses,
> Thy cap, thy kirtle, and thy posies,
> Soon break, soon wither, soon forgotten,
> In folly ripe, in reason rotten.
>
> Thy belt of straw and ivy buds,
> Thy coral clasps and amber studs –
> All those in me no means can move
> To come to thee and be thy love.
>
> But could youth last, and love still breed;
> Had joys no date, nor age no need;
> Then these delights my mind might move
> To live with thee and be thy love.

In the eclogue form itself, perhaps the most vital and original contribution is that of **Michael Drayton** (1563–1631). This prolific poet included a number of pastorals in various of the volumes of verse which he published. There is an element of rustic realism in his eclogues, which distinguishes them from the idealizing Spenserian tradition:

B

BATTE

Gorbo, as thou cam'st this way
By yonder little hill,
Or as thou through the fields didst stray
Saw'st thou my daffadill?

She's in a frock of Lincoln green,
Which colour likes her sight,
And never hath her beauty seen
But through a veil of white.

Than roses richer to behold
That trim up lovers' bowers,
The pansy and the marigold,
Though Phoebus' paramours.

GORBO

Thou well describ'st the daffadill;
It is not full an hour
Since by the spring near yonder hill
I saw that lovely flower.

BATTE

Yet my fair flower thou didst not meet
Nor news of her didst bring,
And yet my Daffadill's more sweet
Than that by yonder spring.

GORBO

I saw a shepherd, that doth keep
In yonder field of lilies,
Was making (as he fed his sheep)
A wreath of daffadillies.

BATTE

Yet, Gorbo, thou delud'st me still;
My flower thou didst not see,
For, know, my pretty daffadill
Is worn of none but me.

To show itself but near her feet
No lily is so bold,
Except to shade her from the heat
Or keep her from the cold.

GORBO

Through yonder vale as I did pass,
Descending from the hill,
I met a smirking bonny lass;
They call her Daffadill.

Whose presence as along she went
The pretty flowers did greet
As though their heads they downward bent
With homage to her feet.

And all the shepherds that were nigh
From top of every hill
Unto the valleys loud did cry
'There goes sweet Daffadill'.

BATTE

Ay, gentle shepherd, now with joy
Thou all my flocks dost fill;
That's she alone, kind shepherd's boy;
Let us to Daffadill.

In *The Shepherd's Sirena* we find the conventional love-lorn shepherd, Dorilus, mourning for his absent Sirena. But, by contrast, his companions are real English shepherds:

Nimble Tom, sirnam'd the Tup,
For his pipe without a peer,
And could tickle Trenchmore up
As 'twould joy your heart to hear;
Ralph, as much renown'd for skill,
That the tabor touch'd so well;
For his gittern little Gill,
That all other did excel;
Rock and Rollo every way
Who still led the rustic ging,
And could troll a roundelay
That would make the fields to ring;
Colin on his shawm so clear
Many a high-pitch'd note that had
And could make the echoes near
Shout as they were waxen mad.

Drayton's last set of eclogues (which he fancifully calls 'Nymphals') is *The Muses Elysium*. Here the setting is a purely imaginary pastoral Elysium, where Drayton can give his Elizabethan fancy full rein. In the second nymphal the shepherds Lalus and Cleon woo the nymph Lirope **with** gifts of a lamb and a kid, sparrows and a dove, flowers and jewels, **and** then offer her a chariot and a boat:

LALUS

When thou shalt please to stem the flood
(As thou art of the wat'ry brood)
I'll have twelve swans more white than snow
Yok'd for the purpose, two and two,
To draw thy barge wrought of fine reed
So well that it nought else shall need.
The traces by which they shall hale
Thy barge shall be the winding trail
Of Woodbine whose brave tassel'd flowers
(The sweetness of the wood-nymphs' bowers)
Shall be the trappings to adorn
The swans by which your barge is borne.
Of flowered flags I'll rob the bank,
Of water cans and king-cups rank,
To be the covering of thy boat;
And, on the stream as thou dost float,
The Naiades that haunt the deep
Themselves about thy barge shall keep,
Recording most delightful lays
By sea-gods written in thy praise.
And in what place thou hapst to land,
There the gentle, silvery sand
Shall soften, curled with the air
As sensible of thy repair.
This, my dear love, I'll do for thee
So thou'lt leave him and go with me.

CLEON

Tush, nymph, his swans will prove but geese,
His barge drinks water like a fleece.
A boat is base: I'll thee provide
A chariot wherein Jove may ride:
In which when bravely thou art borne
Thou shalt look like the glorious morn
Ushering the sun, and such a one
As to this day was never known;
Of the rarest Indian gums
More precious than your balsamums
Which I by art have made so hard

That they with tools may well be carv'd
To make a coach of; which shall be
Materials of this one for thee;
And of thy chariot each small piece
Shall inlaid be with ambergris
And gilded with the yellow ore
Produc'd from Tagus wealthy shore:
In which along the pleasant lawn
With twelve white stags thou shalt be drawn,
Whose branched palms of a stately height
With several nosegays shall be dight,
And as thou rid'st thy coach about
For thy strong guard shall run a rout
Of ostriches, whose curled plumes
'Cens'd with thy chariot's rich perfumes
The scent into the air shall throw;
Whose naked thighs shall grace the show,
Whilst the woodnymphs and those bred
Upon the mountains, o'er thy head
Shall bear a canopy of flowers
Tinsell'd with drops of April showers
Which shall make more glorious shows
Than spangles or your silver oars.
This, bright nymph, I'll do for thee,
So thou'lt leave him and go with me.

Given the dramatic form of the Theocritean idyll, and the essentially dramatic quality of the Renaissance imagination, it was a natural step to write, instead of a series of eclogues, a complete play in which the pastoral dialogues are welded together and given a unified plot. This step was taken in Italy by **Tasso** (1544–95) in his *Aminta*, and by **Guarini** (1537–1612) in his *Il Pastor Fido*. A new form, the Pastoral Drama, was thus created. Its influence can be seen in **Shakespeare** (1564–1616), in *As You Like It* and the Bohemia scenes of *A Winter's Tale*, and also in the unfinished play *The Sad Shepherd* by **Ben Jonson** (1572–1637). This, like *As You Like It*, is partly a sophisticated descendant of the Whitsuntide pastorals, for it introduces Robin Hood and his men, with Maid Marian, rubbing shoulders with Arcadian shepherds in Sherwood Forest. This play shows Jonson in a lyrical and romantic mood far removed from that of his realistic and satirical comedies. We quote the opening soliloquy of the shepherd Æglamour, whose love, Earine, is believed drowned, but in fact has been imprisoned in a hollow tree by the enchantments of the witch Maudlin:

> Here she was wont to go! And here! and here!
> Just where those daisies, pinks and violets grow:
> The world may find the spring by following her,
> For other print her airy steps ne'er left.
> Her treading would not bend a blade of grass,
> Or shake the downy blow-ball from his stalk!
> But like the soft west wind she shot along,
> And where she went, the flowers took thickest root,
> As she had sowed them with her odorous foot.

In *As You Like It* the theme of the conflict between the corrupt life of the court and the natural innocence of rural life is prominent. At the same time the pastoral convention is gently mocked in the persons of Sylvius and Phoebe, and set against the genuine rustic realism of Audrey and William. In *A Winter's Tale* the pastoral world of Bohemia is set against the corruption of the court of Sicilia. It is in this innocent world that the love of Florizel and Perdita can grow, whereby the sin of Leontes is redeemed.

For the union of the actual and the ideal, which is perhaps the fundamental secret of pastoral poetry, the scene of the sheep-shearing feast in the fourth act of Shakespeare's *A Winter's Tale* is beyond comparison. We may quote the old Shepherd's speech to Perdita:

> Fie, daughter! when my old wife lived, upon
> This day she was both pantler, butler, cook,
> Both dame and servant; welcomed all, served all;
> Would sing her song and dance her turn; now here,
> At upper end o' th' table, now i' th' middle,
> On his shoulder, and his; her face o' fire
> With labour and the thing she took to quench it
> She would to each one sip. You are retired,
> As if you were a feasted one and not
> The hostess of the meeting. Pray you, bid
> These unknown friends to's welcome; for it is
> A way to make us better friends, more known.
> Come, quench your blushes and present yourself
> That which you are, mistress o' th' feast. Come on,
> And bid us welcome to your sheep-shearing,
> As your good flock shall prosper.

The most complete reproduction in English, however, of the Italian type of pastoral drama is *The Faithful Shepherdess* by **John Fletcher** (1579–1625). It is a highly artificial, somewhat precious play, but

contains verse of great lyrical beauty. Some of the best of this is given to
the character of the Satyr:

> Here be grapes whose lusty blood
> Is the learned poet's good;
> Sweeter yet did never crown
> The head of Bacchus; nuts more brown
> Than the squirrel's teeth that crack them;
> Deign, O fairest fair, to take them!
> For these black-eyed Driope
> Hath oftentimes commanded me
> With my clasped knee to climb:
> See how well the lusty time
> Hath deck'd their rising cheeks in red,
> Such as on your lips is spread!
> Here be berries for a queen,
> Some be red, some be green;
> These are of that luscious meat
> The great god Pan himself doth eat:
> All these, and what the woods can yield,
> The hanging mountain or the field,
> I freely offer, and ere long
> Will bring you more, more sweet and strong;
> Till when, humbly leave I take,
> Lest the great Pan do awake,
> That sleeping lies in a deep glade,
> Under a broad beech's shade.
> I must go, I must run
> Swifter than the fiery sun.

3

The Seventeenth Century

The intellectual tone of the seventeenth century was, by and large, stronger and more masculine than that of the sixteenth. **John Donne** (1571 or 1572–1631) followed Raleigh in replying somewhat astringently to Marlowe's Passionate Shepherd, in *The Bait*:

> Come live with me, and be my love,
> And we will some new pleasures prove
> Of golden sands, and crystal brooks,
> With silken lines, and silver hooks.
>
> There will the river whisp'ring run
> Warm'd by thine eyes, more than the sun;
> And there th' enamour'd fish will stay,
> Begging themselves they may betray.
>
> When thou wilt swim in that live bath,
> Each fish, which every channel hath,
> Will amorously to thee swim,
> Gladder to catch thee, than thou him.
>
> If thou, to be so seen, be'st loth,
> By sun or moon, thou dark'nest both,
> And if myself have leave to see,
> I need not their light, having thee.
>
> Let others freeze with angling reeds,
> And cut their legs with shells and weeds,
> Or treacherously poor fish beset,
> With strangling snare, or windowy net.
>
> Let coarse bold hands from slimy nest
> The bedded fish in banks out-wrest;
> Or curious traitors, sleeve-silk flies,
> Bewitch poor fishes' wand'ring eyes.
>
> For thee, thou need'st no such deceit,
> For thou thyself art thine own bait:
> That fish, that is not catch'd thereby,
> Alas! is wiser far than I.

Donne is definitely quizzing the convention here; nevertheless it continued to be popular. In this chapter we shall examine certain poets who played their individual baroque variations on the theme.

William Browne (1591–1643) of Tavistock belongs essentially to the earlier Elizabethan tradition. He was a friend of Drayton and Ben Jonson and a follower of Sidney and Spenser. He published *Britannia's Pastorals*, a long rambling pastoral romance in ten-syllable couplets interspersed with lyrics, and a set of eclogues, *The Shepherd's Pipe*. Apart from his admirable epitaphs (such as that on his wife, and on the Countess of Pembroke) he is a diffuse poet, and therefore difficult to quote from. The opening lines of the first eclogue in *The Shepherd's Pipe* may give a sufficient idea of his style:

> Roget, droop not, see the spring
> Is the earth enamelling,
> And the birds on every tree
> Greet this morn with melody:
> Hark, how yonder thrustle chants it,
> And her mate as proudly vaunts it;
> See how every stream is dress'd
> By her margin with the best
> Of Flora's gifts; she seems glad
> For such brooks such flow'rs she had.
> All the trees are quaintly tired
> With green buds, of all desired;
> And the hawthorn every day
> Spreads some little show of May:
> See the primrose sweetly set
> By the much-lov'd violet,
> All the banks do sweetly cover,
> As they would invite a lover
> With his lass to see their dressing
> And to grace them by their pressing.

Browne has a feeling for nature, and especially for the landscape and traditions of his native Devonshire. He appealed to the Romantic taste of the nineteenth century, and influenced Keats. But it was the relaxed self-indulgent Keats of the *Endymion* period.

Phineas Fletcher (1582–1650), a cousin of John Fletcher, is, like his brother Giles, self-consciously Spenserian. He is principally known for his curious allegorical poem, *The Purple Island*. But his *Piscatorie Eclogues* have the original feature that the interlocutors, instead of being shepherds, are fishermen.[1] In the seventh eclogue shepherds and fishermen meet to engage in a singing contest:

> Scarce were the shepherds set, but straight in sight
> The fisher-boyes came driving up the stream;
> Themselves in blue, and twenty sea-nymphs bright
> In curious robes, that well the waves might seem:
> All dark below, the top like frothy cream:
> Their boats and masts with flowres, and garlands dight;
> And round the swannes guard them with armies white:
> Their skiffes by couples dance to sweetest sounds,
> Which running cornets breath to full plain grounds,
> That strikes the river's face, and thence more sweet rebounds.

On the whole these poems are marked by elaborate rhetoric rather than any fresh feeling for nature. With some ingenuity Fletcher makes the images of sea and river-bank reflect the love-passions of his fishermen, as those of fields and woods do for the shepherds of the more traditional pastorals:

> You steady rocks, why still do you stand still?
> You fleeting waves, why do you never stand?
> *Amyntas* hath forgot his *Thelgon's* quill;
> His promise, and his love are writ in sand:
> But rocks are firm, though *Neptune* rage his fill;
> When thou, *Amyntas*, like the fire-drake rangest:
> The sea keeps on his course, when like the winde thou changest.

Fletcher follows Spenser in making the pastoral a vehicle for allegorical autobiography and for ecclesiastical satire. The references to Russia, which his father, Giles Fletcher the elder, had been one of the first Englishmen to visit and to give an account of, are of some historical interest:

> From thence he furrow'd many a churlish sea,
> The viny *Rhene* and *Volgha's* self did passe,
> Who sleds doth suffer on his watry lea,
> And horses trampling on his ycie face:
> Where *Phoebus* prison'd in the frozen glasse,
> All winter cannot move his quenched light,

---

[1] Phineas Fletcher also wrote a pastoral drama, or rather, as he himself calls it, 'a piscatory', *Sicelides*. Fishing seems to have had a special fascination for the seventeenth century — cf. Donne's *The Bait*, quoted above, and the popularity of Walton's *Compleat Angler*. This latter work bears some relation to the pastoral. Theocritus had introduced fishermen as the speakers in his twenty-first idyll; but Fletcher's immediate model is the Italian writer **Sannazaro**, whose piscatory eclogues appeared in 1526.

> Nor in the heat will drench his chariot bright:
> Thereby the tedious years is all one day and night.

In using the life of the fisherman as a basis for Christian allegory, Fletcher
has, of course, as good a precedent in the New Testament as the pastoralists
who followed Mantuan had in using that of the shepherd — since the first
Apostles were fishermen whom Christ commanded to become fishers of
men. Fletcher's religious sympathies are Puritan and antiprelatical. In
the following passage he thus denounces the Anglican clergy of his day:

> Little know they the fishers toilsome pain,
> Whose labour with his age, still growing, spends not:
> His care and watchings (oft misspent in vain)
> The early morn begins, dark evening ends not.
> > Too foolish men, that think all labour stands
> > In travell of the feet, and tired hands!
> >   .   .   .   .

> Instead of these a crue of idle grooms,
> Idle, and bold, that never saw the seas,
> Fearlesse succeed, and fill their empty rooms:
> Some lazy live, bathing in wealth and ease:
> > Their floating boats with waves have leave to play,
> > Their rusty hooks all yeare keep holy-day.

> Here stray their skiffes, themselves are never here,
> Ne'er saw their boats: ill mought they fishers be:
> Mean time some wanton boy the boat doth steer,
> (Poor boat the while!) that cares as much as he:
> > Who in a brook a whirry cannot row,
> > Now backs the seas, before the seas he know.
> >   .   .   .   .

> Some stretching in their boats supinely sleep,
> Seasons in vain recall'd, and windes neglecting:
> Others their hooks and baits in poison steep,
> *Neptune* himself with deathfull drugges infecting:
> > The fish their life and death together drink,
> > And dead pollute the seas with venom'd stink.
> >   .   .   .   .

> Some greater, scorning now their narrow boat,
> In mighty hulks and ships (like courts) do dwell;
> Slaving the skiffes that in their seas do float;
> Their silken sails with windes do proudly swell;
> > Their narrow bottomes stretch they large and wide,
> > And make full room for luxurie and pride.

Fletcher is here striking at the abuse of absenteeism, and at the Laudian bishops whom he accuses of infecting Charles I (Neptune) with their Arminian doctrines.

These passages anticipate St. Peter's speech in Milton's *Lycidas*. **Milton** (1608–74) was influenced by both the Fletcher brothers, and his starting point, like theirs, was in the Cambridge Spenserian tradition. With the examples of Spenser and Virgil, the pastoral was now coming to be thought of as a suitable testing-ground for a poet of epic ambitions. Milton seems to have regarded most of his early verse as more or less pastoral in character, though he did not write a set of formal eclogues. In the *Hymn on the Morning of Christ's Nativity* he treats the scene of the Annunciation to the Shepherds in the pastoral manner:

> The Shepherds on the Lawn,
> Or ere the point of dawn,
>   Sate simply chatting in a rustick row;
> Full little thought they than,
> That the mighty *Pan*
>   Was kindly com to live with them below;
> Perhaps their loves, or els their sheep,
> Was all that did their silly thoughts so busie keep.
>
> When such musick sweet
> Their hearts and ears did greet,
>   As never was by mortall finger strook,
> Divinely-warbl'd voice
> Answering the stringed noise,
>   As all their souls in blisfull rapture took:
> The air such pleasure loth to lose,
> With thousand echo's still prolongs each heav'nly close.

The identification of Pan here, as also sometimes in Spenser, with the universal god, was made possible by the supposed etymology of the name from Greek *pan* = all.

Arcadian pastoral names are introduced into the English rustic land-scape of *L'Allegro*:

> Hard by, a Cottage chimney smokes,
> From betwixt two aged Okes,
> Where *Corydon* and *Thyrsis* met,
> Are at their savory dinner set
> Of Hearbs, and other Country Messes,
> Which the neat-handed *Phillis* dresses;

> And then in haste her Bowre she leaves,
> With *Thestylis* to bind the Sheaves.

Milton's two masques, though otherwise very different, are both pastoral in character. *Arcades* consists of little more than a couple of songs, of which we quote the second:

> Nymphs and Shepherds dance no more
>   By sandy *Ladons* Lillied banks.
> On old *Lycaeus* or *Cyllene* hoar,
>   Trip no more in twilight ranks,
> Though *Erymanth* your loss deplore,
>   A better soyl shall give ye thanks.
> From the stony *Maenalus*,
> Bring your Flocks, and live with us,
> Here ye shall have greater grace,
> To serve the Lady of this place.
>   Though *Syrinx* your *Pans* Mistres were,
>   Yet *Syrinx* well may wait on her.
>   Such a rural Queen
>   All *Arcadia* hath not seen.

Comus on the other hand is a full-scale dramatic fable. It learnedly echoes Greek drama, with its Euripidean prologue and its stichomythia, but also shows the influence of the Italian pastoral drama. Its plot is probably drawn from an English folk-tale, which had been used by George Peele in his play *The Old Wives' Tale*, a variant of Childe Roland. The Attendant Spirit disguises himself as the shepherd Thyrsis, whom the elder brother thus addresses:

> *Thyrsisv*, Whose artful strains have oft delaid
> The huddling brook to hear his madrigal,
> And sweeten'd every muskrose of the dale,
> How cam'st thou here good Swain? hath any ram
> Slip't from the fold, or young Kid lost his dam,
> Or straggling weather the pen't flock forsook?
> How couldst thou find this dark sequester'd nook?

Lycidas is a pastoral elegy on the model of Moschus's *Lament for Bion*, but also has Virgilian echoes. Its subject is Milton's Cambridge contemporary Edward King, who was drowned while on a voyage to Ireland. It was originally a contribution to a memorial volume which King's friends brought out. It does not seem that King was a particularly intimate friend of Milton's. Nevertheless King's death led Milton to consider two subjects with which he was deeply concerned – his own destiny as a poet, and the contemporary state of the English church.

These two subjects are treated in what are in effect episodes, departing from the pastoral manner of the poem as a whole. The early and unforeseen death of King, who had shown promise as a poet, leads Milton to consider the possibility of his own early death (the more as he was also about to undertake a voyage overseas to Italy) and to ask the question:

> Alas! What boots it with uncessant care
> To tend the homely slighted Shepherd's trade,
> And strictly meditate the thankless Muse,
> Were it not better done, as others use,
> To sport with *Amaryllis* in the shade,
> Or with the tangles of *Neæra's* hair?
> *Fame* is the spur that the clear spirit doth raise
> (That last infirmity of Noble mind)
> To scorn delights, and live laborious dayes;
> But the fair Guerdon when we hope to find,
> And think to burst out into sudden blaze,
> Comes the blind *Fury* with th' abhorred shears,
> And slits the thin-spun life. . .

The voice that replies is that of the god of poetry, Phoebus himself:

> *Fame* is no plant that grows on mortal soil,
> Nor in the glistering foil
> Set off to th' world, nor in broad rumour lies,
> But lives and spreds aloft by those pure eyes,
> And perfet witnes of all-judging *Jove*;
> As he pronounces lastly on each deed,
> Of so much fame in Heav'n expect thy meed.

Though their language is pagan and classical, these lines spring from Milton's Christian faith that the ways of God are just, and justifiable to man. This, and with it the related theme of choice and commitment of life, were to be central to Milton's two epic poems and culminate in his tragedy, *Samson Agonistes*. They are thus associated in Milton's mind with the sphere of epic and tragic poetry, and require a deliberate return to the level of pastoral poetry:

> O Fountain *Arethuse*, and thou honour'd floud,
> Smooth-sliding *Mincius*, crown'd with vocall reeds,
> That strain I heard was of a higher mood:
> But now my Oate proceeds . . .

The Sicilian fountain of Arethuse and the Italian river Mincius deliberately reinvoke the pastoral worlds of Theocritus and Virgil respectively. This leads on to the traditional procession of mourning figures – the herald of the seas, Camus (the river Cam, representing the University of Cambridge) and, finally, St. Peter, 'The pilot of the Galilean lake'. Here the tone modulates once again, as St. Peter denounces the Laudian clergy. This is in the tradition of allegorical ecclesiastical satire, stemming from Mantuan. But it has a weight and seriousness beyond anything Googe, Spenser, or Phineas Fletcher achieved:

> How well could I have spar'd for thee, young swain,
> Anow of such as for their bellies sake,
> Creep and intrude, and climb into the fold!
> Of other care they little reck'ning make,
> Then how to scramble at the shearers feast
> And shove away the worthy bidden guest;
> Blind mouthes! that scarce themselves know how to hold
> A Sheep-hook, or have learn'd ought els the least
> That to the faithful Herdmans art belongs!
> What recks it them? What need they? They are sped;
> And when they list, their lean and flashy songs
> Grate on their scrannel Pipes of wretched straw,
> The hungry Sheep look up, and are not fed,
> But, swoln with wind and the rank mist they draw,
> Rot inwardly, and foul contagion spread:
> Besides what the grim Woolf with privy paw
> Daily devours apace, and nothing sed,
> But that two-handed engine at the door,
> Stands ready to smite once, and smite no more.

King had in fact been intending to take Holy Orders. The deliberate harshness and obscurity of language in this passage is meant, I think, to sign-post us that we are now moving on the level of satire. In the early seventeenth-century, before the advent of Dryden, it was precisely this kind of language which satirists like Donne and Marston employed, following the Latin examples of Juvenal and Persius. Milton has therefore to invoke yet again, the pastoral muse, and the river Alpheus, which was supposed to run underground in pursuit of the fountain nymph Arethusa, to re-emerge in Sicily:

> Return *Alpheus*, the dread voice is past,
> That shrunk thy streams; Return *Sicilian* Muse . . .

The decorative beauty of the floral passage which follows, not only re-establishes the pastoral world, and compensates for the harshness of what preceded it, but almost lulls us into a conventional acceptance of death. But then it is interrupted by the poignant remembrance of the reality of loss:

> Ay me! Whilst thee the shores, and sounding Seas
> Wash far away, where ere thy bones are hurld,
> Whether beyond the stormy *Hebrides*,
> Where thou perhaps under the whelming tide
> Visit'st the bottom of the monstrous world . . .

The final section of the poem (apart from the last stanza, which we may regard as a coda) is a double apotheosis. For it includes both a vision of the Christian Heaven with the almost Dantesque line — That sing, and singing in their glory move — and the pagan and classical conception of Lycidas transformed into the Genius of the Shore.

The great complexity of tone in *Lycidas*, some of which we have tried to indicate above, is matched by its metrical form. It consists of a series of irregular stanzas, containing five-stressed and three-stressed lines intermixed, mostly rhymed but sometimes left blank. This, as Professor F. T. Prince has pointed out, probably derived from the Italian *canzone libera* as used in the pastoral dramas of Tasso and Guarini. But the final stanza is in the regular *ottava rima*. In this coda Milton moves from the first to the third person; the shifting and conflicting emotions of the poem are as it were distanced and set in a static frame. The uncouth swain twitches his mantle blue — 'Tomorrow to fresh Woods, and Pastures new' — a reference perhaps to Milton's intended continental tour; but also a farewell to pastoral poetry and an indication that Milton now aspired to more ambitious forms.

A very individual version of the pastoral theme is presented by **Andrew Marvell** (1621–78) in a group of four poems in which the speaker, instead of the conventional shepherd, is The Mower:

> I am the mower *Damon*, known
> Through all the meadows I have mown.
> On me the morn her dew distils
> Before her darling daffodils;
> And, if at noon my toil me heat,
> The sun himself licks off my sweat;
> While, going home, the ev'ning sweet
> In cowslip-water bathes my feet.

What though the piping shepherd stock
The plains with an unnumb'red flock,
This scythe of mine discovers wide
More ground than all his sheep do hide.
With this the golden fleece I shear
Of all these closes ev'ry year.
And though in wool more pure than they,
Yet I am richer far in hay.

Nor am I so deform'd to sight,
If in my scythe I lookéd right;
In which I see my picture done,
As in a crescent moon the sun.
The deathless fairies take me oft
To lead them in their dances soft;
And when I tune myself to sing,
About me they contract their ring.

How happy might I still have mow'd,
Had not Love here his thistle sow'd!
But now I all the day complain,
Joining my labour to my pain;
And with my scythe cut down the grass,
Yet still my grief is where it was;
But, when the iron blunter grows,
Sighing I whet my scythe and woes.

While thus he drew his elbow round,
Depopulating all the ground,
And, with his whistling scythe, does cut
Each stroke between the earth and root,
The edgéd steel, by careless chance,
Did into his own ankle glance,
And there among the grass fell down,
By his own scythe the mower mown.

Alas! said he, these hurts are slight
To those that die by Love's despite.
With shepherd's purse, and clown's all-heal
The blood I stanch and wound I seal.
Only for him no cure is found,
Whom JULIANA'S eyes do wound.
'Tis Death alone that this must do:
For, Death, thou art a Mower too.

The final conceit on Death is highly characteristic of the Metaphysical School. This extract is from the second of the Mower poems, *Damon the Mower*. The others are *The Mower Against Gardens*, *The Mower to the Glow-Worms*, and *The Mower's Song*. They are all typical of Marvell's style, combining an ironic use of the conceit with a personal and almost pre-Romantic feeling for nature.

The poets of the Restoration period continued to employ the pastoral convention, at least in using pastoral names when celebrating their mistresses. But, by and large, they are remote from the pastoral world. It is as if they are quite at home in urban sophisticated society, and have not yet reached the nostalgia for rural innocence which marks the eighteenth century. A typical piece of Restoration wit with a pseudo-pastoral setting is *Phillis Knotting*, by **Sir Charles Sedley** (?1639–1701):

Hears not my *Phillis*, how the birds
    Their feather'd Mates salute?
They tell their Passion in their Words;
    Must I alone be mute;
Phillis, *without Frown or Smile*,
Sat and knotted all the while.

The God of Love in thy bright Eyes
    Does like a Tyrant reign;
But in thy Heart a Child he lyes,
    Without his Dart or Flame.
Phillis, *without Frown or Smile*,
Sat and knotted all the while.

So many Months in Silence past,
    And yet in raging Love,
Might well deserve one Word at last,
    My Passion shou'd approve.
Phillis, *without Frown or Smile*,
Sat and knotted all the while.

Must then your faithful Swain expire,
    And not one look obtain,
Which he, to sooth his fond Desire,
    Might pleasingly explain?
Phillis, *without Frown or Smile*
Sat and knotted all the while.

There is, however, some good pastoral verse in a place where we might not expect to find it – in the heroic sub-plot of the witty and cynical comedy *Marriage à la Mode* by **John Dryden** (1631–1700). Leonidas and Palmyra, who though of princely rank have been brought up as shepherds, are now at court, and describe their old life and how they first fell in love:

> *Palmyra.* Do you remember, when their tasks were done,
> How all the youth did to our cottage run?
> While winter-winds were whistling loud without,
> Our cheerful hearth was circled round about:
> With strokes in ashes, maids their lovers drew;
> And still you fell to me, and I to you.
>
> *Leonidas.* When love did of my heart possession take,
> I was so young, my soul was scarce awake:
> I cannot tell when first I thought you fair;
> But sucked in love, insensibly as air.
>
> *Palmyra.* I know too well when first my love began,
> When at our wake you for the chaplet ran:
> Then I was made the lady of the May,
> And, with the garland, at the goal did stay:
> Still, as you ran, I kept you full in view;
> I hoped, and wished, and ran, methought, for you.
> As you came near, I hastily did rise,
> And stretched my arm outright, that held the prize.
> The custom was to kiss whom I should crown;
> You kneeled, and in my lap your head laid down:
> I blushed, and blushed, and did the kiss delay;
> At last my subjects forced me to obey:
> But, when I gave the crown, and then the kiss,
> I scarce had breath to say, Take that, — and this.

We shall conclude this chapter, however, with Dryden's *The Lady's Song*. This pastoral lyric, written by the old poet after the revolution of 1688, is in fact an inflammatory summons to the Jacobite party to resort to force. Pan is James II, Syrinx is his Queen, Mary of Modena, and their son is the infant prince who was to become the Old Pretender. One can imagine the effect that this daring little poem might have had if sung at a private music-gathering. But there is also an undercurrent of feeling in it as Dryden looks back at a vanished world which in his heart he knows is gone forever:

> A quire of bright Beauties in Spring did appear,
> To chuse a *May*-lady to govern the Year;
> All the Nymphs were in White, and the Shepherds in Green,

The Garland was giv'n, and *Phillis* was Queen;
But *Phillis* refus'd it, and sighing did say,
I'll not wear a garland while *Pan* is away.

While *Pan*, and fair *Syrinx*, are fled from our Shore,
The Graces are banish'd, and Love is no more:
The soft God of Pleasure that warm'd our Desires,
Has broken his Bow, and extinguish'd his Fires;
And vows that himself, and his Mother, will mourn,
Till *Pan* and fair *Syrinx* in Triumph return.

Forbear your Addresses, and Court us no more,
For we will perform what the Deity swore:
But, if you dare think of deserving our Charms,
Away with your Sheephooks, and take to your Arms;
Then Lawrels and Myrtles your Brows shall adorn,
When *Pan*, and his Son, and fair *Syrinx* return.

4

The Eighteenth Century

Everyone has heard how Marie Antoinette had a dairy house built for herself in the grounds of Le Petit Trianon, whither, when fatigued with the formalities of Versailles, she and her ladies could retire, and, dressed as shepherdesses, indulge the fancy of pastoral simplicity. This represents very well the eighteenth-century attitude to the pastoral as a poetic form – one which in this century became yet again extremely popular. The same fashion is typified by the Dresden figures of shepherds and shepherdesses which were produced at this period. Such things still probably affect the image which the general reader has of the pastoral, as a purely artificial and rather precious form – though as we have seen, it is in fact capable of a much wider interpretation, and could be used for more serious poetical purposes.

The pastorals of **Alexander Pope** (1688–1744) were his first published work. He claimed that they were written at the age of sixteen; there is no reason to question this, though they were doubtless touched-up when they appeared in 1709. Pope prefaced them with a discourse on pastoral poetry, in which he thus defines his intentions:

The original of Poetry is ascribed to that Age which succeeded the creation of the world: and as the keeping of flocks seems to have been the first employment of mankind, the most ancient sort of poetry was probably *pastoral*. It is natural to imagine, that the leisure of those ancient shepherds admitting and inviting some diversion, none was so proper to that solitary and sedentary life as singing; and that in their songs they took occasion to celebrate their own felicity. From hence a Poem was invented, and afterwards improv'd to a perfect image of that happy time; which by giving us an esteem for the virtues of a former age, might recommend them to the present. And since the life of shepherds was attended with more tranquillity than any other rural employment, the Poets chose to introduce their Persons, from whom it receiv'd the name of Pastoral.

A Pastoral is an imitation of the action of a shepherd, or one considered under that character. The form of this imitation is dramatic, or narrative, or mix'd of both; the fable simple, the manners not too polite nor too rustic: the thoughts are plain, yet admit a little quickness and passion, but that short and flowing: the expression humble, yet as pure as the language will afford; neat, but not florid; easy, and yet lively. In short, the fable, manners, thoughts, and expressions are full of the greatest simplicity in nature.

The complete character of this Poem consists in simplicity, brevity, and delicacy; the two first of which render an eclogue natural, and the last delightful.

If we would copy Nature, it may be useful to take this Idea along with us, that Pastoral is an image of what they call the Golden Age.

From this it must appear that Pope's aim is purely artistic and ideal. It would be absurd to look for any element of realism in these poems, though they are not without touches of genuine observation of nature. The Pastorals are four in number, and Pope imitates Spenser's scheme in *The Shepheard's Calender* by adapting them to the four seasons of the year. That Pope regarded himself as the legitimate successor of Spenser is made especially clear in the second pastoral: *Summer*. This is a monologue by the shepherd Alexis, whose name is an adaptation of Pope's own christian name. Its first line echoes the opening line of Spenser's January Æglogue:

> A Shepherd's Boy (he seeks no better Name)
> Led forth his Flocks along the silver *Thame*,
> Where dancing Sun-beams on the Waters play'd,
> And verdant Alders form'd a quiv'ring Shade.
> Soft as he mourn'd, the Streams forgot to flow,
> The Flocks around a dumb Compassion show,
> The *Naiads* wept in ev'ry Watry Bow'r,
> And *Jove* consented in a silent Show'r.

Later on Spenser is specifically referred to as Colin:

> That Flute is mine which *Colin's* tuneful Breath
> Inspir'd when living, and bequeath'd in Death;
> He said: *Alexis*, take this Pipe, the same
> That taught the Groves my *Rosalinda's* Name –

In the same poem occur the following beautiful lines, which must be familiar to many who do not know their source:

> Where'er you walk, cool Gales shall fan the Glade,
> Trees, where you sit, shall crowd into a Shade:
> Where'er you tread, the blushing Flow'rs shall rise,
> And all things flourish where you turn your Eyes.

These words were set by Handel, and introduced as an aria in his opera *Semele*, the libretto of which is by Congreve.

Within the limits which Pope set himself, the pastorals exhibit extraordinary virtuosity. They are marked by a delicately sensuous imagery, and above all by the musical quality of the verse. Pope shows that he can give to his chosen form, the heroic couplet, a lyrical character when he wishes. This is perhaps best exhibited in the elegy for Daphne in the Fourth Pastoral: *Winter*. One should also note the skill with which in each stanza a key word is picked up and introduced to vary the refrain:

> Ye gentle *Muses*, leave your Chrystal Spring,
> Let *Nymphs* and *Sylvans* Cypress Garlands bring;
> Ye weeping *Loves*, the Stream with Myrtles hide,
> And break your Bows, as when *Adonis* dy'd;
> And with your Golden Darts, now useless grown,
> Inscribe a Verse on this relenting Stone:
> 'Let Nature change, let Heav'n and Earth deplore,
> Fair *Daphne's* dead, and Love is now no more!'
>
> 'Tis done, and Nature's various Charms decay;
> See gloomy Clouds obscure the chearful Day!
> Now hung with Pearls the dropping Trees appear,
> Their faded Honours scatter'd on her Bier.
> See, where on Earth the flow'ry Glories lye,
> With her they flourish'd, and with her they dye.
> Ah what avail the Beauties Nature wore?
> Fair *Daphne's* dead, and Beauty is no more!
>
> For her, the Flocks refuse their verdant Food,
> The thirsty Heifers shun the gliding Flood.
> The silver Swans her hapless Fate bemoan,
> In Notes more sad than when they sing their own.
> In hollow Caves sweet *Echo* silent lies,
> Silent, or only to her Name replies,
> Her Name with Pleasure once she taught the Shore,
> Now *Daphne's* dead, and Pleasure is no more!
>
> No grateful Dews descend from Ev'ning Skies,
> Nor Morning Odours from the Flow'rs arise.
> No rich Perfumes refresh the fruitful Field,
> Nor fragrant Herbs their native Incense yield.
> The balmy *Zephyrs*, silent since her Death,
> Lament the Ceasing of a sweeter Breath.
> Th' industrious Bees neglect their Golden Store;
> Fair *Daphne's* dead, and Sweetness is no more!
>
> No more the mounting Larks, while *Daphne* sings,
> Shall list'ning in mid air suspend their Wings;
> No more the Birds shall imitate her Lays,
> Or hush'd with Wonder, hearken from the Sprays:
> No more the Streams their Murmurs shall forbear,
> A sweeter Musick than their own to hear,
> But tell the Reeds, and tell the vocal Shore,

Fair *Daphne*'s dead, and Musick is no more!
　Her Fate is whisper'd by the gentle Breeze,
And told in Sighs to all the trembling Trees;
The trembling Trees, in ev'ry Plain and Wood,
Her Fate remurmur to the silver Flood;
The silver Flood, so lately calm, appears
Swell'd with new Passion, and o'erflows with Tears;
The Winds and Trees and Floods her Death deplore,
Daphne, our Grief! our Glory now no more!
　But see! where *Daphne* wond'ring mounts on high,
Above the Clouds, above the Starry Sky.
Eternal Beauties grace the shining Scene,
Fields ever fresh, and Groves for ever green!
There, while you rest in *Amaranthine* Bow'rs,
Or from those Meads select unfading Flow'rs,
Behold us kindly, who your Name implore,
Daphne, our Goddess, and our Grief no more!

Besides this set of pastorals, Pope's poem *The Messiah* also demands attention. This is an imitation of Virgil's *Messianic Eclogue*. Pope accepts the traditional view that Virgil's source was a Sybilline prophecy referring to the coming of Christ, and notes with justice the resemblance between the Latin poet's imagery and certain passages from the book of Isaiah. He therefore attempts to paraphrase these same scriptural passages in a Virgilian style, as here:

Hark! a glad Voice the lonely Desart chears:
Prepare the Way! a God, a God appears.
A God! a God! the vocal Hills reply,
The Rocks proclaim th'approaching Deity.
Lo, Earth receives him from the bending Skies!
Sink down ye Mountains, and ye Vallies rise:
With Heads declin'd, ye Cedars, Homage pay;
Be smooth ye Rocks, ye rapid Floods give way!

This is based on the following verses from *Isaiah* Chap. 40:

The voice of him that crieth in the wilderness, Prepare ye the way of the Lord, make straight in the desert a high way for our God. Every valley shall be exalted, and every mountain and hill shall be made low: and the crooked shall be made straight, and the rough places plain.

The reader may well feel that comparison with the language of the Authorized Version is damaging to Pope. But the experiment is an interesting one, and perhaps the present generation, which has widely accepted a translation of the Scriptures into what some have considered Civil Service English, should not be too ready to sneer.

The Pastorals of **Ambrose Phillips** (1675?–1749) are chiefly remembered for the quarrel they engendered between their author and Pope. Phillips was a member of Addison's circle, who met at Buttons coffee house, a circle which at this early stage of his career Pope also frequented. A series of papers on pastoral poetry appeared in Steele's *Guardian*. Their author was Thomas Tickell, another member of Addison's circle, and in them Phillips's work was praised alongside that of Theocritus, Virgil and Spenser, while Pope's pastorals were ignored. This naturally irritated Pope, who himself contributed to the *Guardian*, No. 40, an anonymous paper, in which Phillips's work and his own were compared. The essay purported to continue to praise Phillips, at the expense of Pope himself. But it was in fact a piece of irony, in which the insipidity of Phillips was shown up by placing passages side by side with parallel passages from Pope's own work:

But the better to discover the Merits of our two Contemporary Pastoral Writers, I shall endeavour to draw a Parallel of them, by setting several of their particular Thoughts in the same light, whereby it will be obvious how much *Phillips* hath the Advantage. With what Simplicity he introduces two Shepherds singing alternately.

> Hobb. *Come*, Rosalind, *O come, for without thee*
> *What Pleasure can the Country have for me:*
> *Come*, Rosalind, *O come; my brinded Kine,*
> *My snowy Sheep, my Farm, and all is thine.*

> Lanq. *Come*, Rosalind, *O come; here shady Bow'rs*
> *Here are cool Fountains, and here springing Flow'rs*
> *Come*, Rosalind; *Here ever let us stay,*
> *And sweetly waste our live-long Time away.*

Our other Pastoral Writer, in expressing the same Thought, deviates into downright Poetry.

> Streph. *In Spring the Fields, in Autumn Hills I love,*
> *At Morn the Plains, at Noon the shady Grove,*
> *But Delia always; forc'ed from Delia's sight,*
> *Nor Plains at Morn, nor Groves at Noon delight.*

> Daph. Sylvia's *like Autumn ripe, yet mild* as May,
> *More bright than Noon, yet fresh as early Day:*
> *Ev'n Spring displeases, when she shines not here.*
> *But blest with her, 'tis Spring throughout the year.*

It is only fair to Phillips to quote something from him other than the passages singled out by Pope. The following, for instance, from his Third Pastoral, an elegy on Albino (the young Duke of Gloucester, the only one of Queen Anne's children to survive infancy) is really quite pretty:

> O now, if ever, bring
> The laurel green, the smelling eglantine,
> And tender branches from the mantling vine;
> The dewy cowslip, that in meadow grows,
> The fountain-violet, and garden-rose,
> Marsh-lilies sweet, and tufts of daffodil,
> With what ye cull from wood, or verdant hill,
> Whether in open sun, or shade they blow,
> More early some, and some unfolding slow.
> Bring in heap'd canisters, of every kind,
> As if the summer had with spring combin'd,
> And nature, forward to assist your care,
> Did not profusion for Albino spare.
> Your hamlets strew, and every public way;
> And consecrate to mirth Albino's day:
> Myself will lavish all my little store,
> And deal about the goblet flowing o'er:
> Old Moulin there shall harp, young Myco sing,
> And Cuddy dance the round amid the ring,
> And Hobbinol his antic gambols play:
> To thee these honours, yearly, will we pay.

Phillips regarded himself as the legitimate heir of Spenser – a position which, as we have seen, Pope also claimed. He gives Spenserian names to his shepherds, instead of the classical ones favoured by Pope, and also copies Spenser's archaising diction. Instead of Pope's classical idealization, his aim is an artless rustic simplicity. Pope's friend **John Gay** (1685–1732), in his *Shepherd's Week*, aimed at continuing Pope's ironic attack on Phillips by parodying these elements in his style. His aim is to press them to their logical conclusion by reproducing the actual coarseness of rustic life. But curiously, Gay's satire overreaches itself. His pastorals have a real vitality and interest which is given to them by this very element. The Proeme, written in pseudo-archaic prose indicates Gay's intentions:

Other Poet travailing in this plain highway of Pastoral know I none. Yet, certes, such it behoveth a Pastoral to be, as nature in the country affordeth; and the manners also meetly copied from the rustical folk therein. In this also my love to my native country Britain much pricketh me forward, to describe aright the manners of our own honest and laborious plough-men, in no wise sure more unworthy a British Poet's imitation, than those of Sicily or Arcadie; albeit, not ignorant I am, what a rout and rabblement of critical gallimawfry hath been made of late days by certain young men of insipid delicacy, concerning, I wist not what, Golden Age, and other outrageous conceits, to which they would confine Pastoral . . .

This idle trumpery (only fit for schools and schoolboys) unto that ancient Doric shepherd Theocritus, or his mates, was never known; he rightly, throughout his fifth Idyll, maketh his louts give foul language, and behold their goats at rut in all simplicity . . .

Thou wilt not find my shepherdesses idly piping on oaten reeds, but milking the kine, tying up the sheaves, or if the hogs are astray driving them to their styes. My shepherd gathereth none other nose-gays but what are the growth of our own fields, he sleepeth not under myrtle shades, but under a hedge, nor doth he vigilantly defend his flocks from wolves, because there are none, as maister Spenser well observeth.

All this is intended ironically, but the fact is that, willy-nilly, Gay is in some ways closer to the real spirit of Theocritus than any other English Pastoralist. Although his intentions are satirical, his imagination, unlike that of his friends Swift and Pope, was essentially an innocent one. He gives absurd names, like Blouzelind and Grubbinol to his shepherds and shepherdesses, but he has closely observed the real manners of the peasants of his native Somerset:

> If in the soil you guide the crooked share,
> Your early breakfast is my constant care;
> And when with even hand you strow the grain,
> I fright the thievish rooks from off the plain.
> In misling days when I my thresher heard,
> With nappy beer I to the barn repair'd;
> Lost in the musick of the whirling flail,
> To gaze on thee I left the smoking pail:
> In harvest when the Sun was mounted high,
> My leathern bottle did thy drought supply;
> When-e'er you mow'd I follow'd with the rake,
> And have full oft been sun-burnt for thy sake;
> When in the welkin gathering show'rs were seen,
> I lagg'd the last with *Colin* on the green;
> And when at eve returning with thy carr,
> Awaiting heard the gingling bells from far;
> Straight on the fire the sooty pot I plac't,
> To warm thy broth I burnt my hands for haste.
> When hungry thou stood'st *staring, like an Oaf,*

> I sliced the luncheon from the barley loaf,
> With crumbled bread I thicken'd well thy mess,
> Ah! love me more, or love thy pottage less!

The death-bed scene of Blouzelind is genuinely touching:

> How shall I, void of tears, her death relate,
> While on her darling's bed her mother sate!
> These words the dying *Blouzelinda* spoke,
> And *of the dead let none the will revoke.*

> Mother, quoth she, let not the poultry need,
> And give the goose wherewith to raise her breed,
> Be these my sister's care — and ev'ry morn
> Amid the ducklings let her scatter corn;
> The sickly calf that's hous'd, be sure to tend,
> Feed him with milk, and from bleak colds defend,
> Yet ere I die — see, mother, yonder shelf,
> There secretly I've hid my worldly pelf.
> Twenty good shillings in a rag I laid,
> Be ten the Parson's, for my sermon paid.
> The rest is yours — my spinning-wheel and rake,
> Let *Susan* keep for her dear sister's sake;
> My new straw hat that's trimly lin'd with green,
> Let *Peggy* wear, for she's a damsel clean.
> My leathern bottle, long in harvests try'd,
> Be *Grubbinol's* — this silver ring beside:
> Three silver pennies, and a nine-pence bent,
> A token kind to *Bumkinet* is sent.
> Thus spoke the maiden, while her mother cry'd,
> And peaceful, like the harmless lamb, she dy'd.

Thursday, or The Spell is modelled on the Simaetha Idyll of Theocritus, but accurately records English folk-beliefs.

Besides *The Shepherd's Week,* Gay wrote several other eclogues in a similarly ironical vein. The *Town Eclogues* (a genre to which **Lady Mary Wortley Montague** (1689–1762) also contributed) are pictures of contemporary fashionable life — *The Toilette, The Card Table* and *The Funeral.* They belong to the same world as Pope's *The Rape of the Lock. A Sober Eclogue* is a satire on the Quakers, but although Gay unjustly imputes to them sexual laxity, they are not unsympathetically presented:

> Ah *Tabitha,* to hear these words of thine,
> My pulse beats high, as if inflam'd with wine!
> When to the brethren first with fervent zeal

The spirit mov'd thy yearnings to reveal,
How did I joy thy trembling lip to see
Red as the cherry from the *Kentish* tree;
When ecstasy had warm'd thy look so meek,
Gardens of roses blushed upon thy cheek!
With what sweet transport didst thou roll thine eyes,
How did thy words provoke the brethren's sighs!
Words that with holy sighs might others move,
But, *Tabitha*, my sighs were sighs of love.

The Birth of the Squire belongs to the rustic world of *The Shepherd's Week*.
It is a parody of Virgil's *Pollio*, or Messianic eclogue, in which the future
exploits of the young hero are foretold:

Beagles and spaniels round his cradle stand,
Kiss his moist lip and gently lick his hand;
He joys to hear the shrill horn's echoing sounds,
And learns to lisp the names of all the hounds.
With frothy ale to make his cup o'erflow,
Barley shall in paternal acres grow;
The bee shall sip the fragrant dew from flow'rs,
To give metheglin for his morning hours;
For him the clustring hop shall climb the poles,
And his own orchard sparkle in his bowls.

. . . .

Ah, too fond mother, think the time draws nigh,
That calls the darling from thy tender eye;
How shall his spirit brook the rigid rules,
And the long tyranny of grammar schools?
Let younger brothers o'er dull authors plod,
Lash'd into *Latin* by the tingling rod,
No, let him never feel that smart disgrace:
Why should he wiser prove than all his race?

When rip'ning youth with down o'ershades his chin,
And ev'ry female eye incites to sin;
The milk-maid (thoughtless of her future shame)
With smacking lip shall rouse his guilty flame;
The dairy, barn, the hay-loft and the grove
Shall oft be conscious of their stolen love.

. . . .

On fam'd *St. Hubert's* feast, his winding horn
Shall cheer the joyful hound and wake the morn:
This memorable day his eager speed
Shall urge with bloody heel the rising steed.

O check the foamy bit, nor tempt thy fate,
Think on the murders of a five-bar gate!

. . . .

He shall survive; and in late years be sent
To snore away debates in *Parliament*.

William Diaper (1685–1717) had the original idea of making the speakers in his *Nereides*, or Sea-Eclogues, mermaids and tritons. This fancy has a certain charm, and allows Diaper to display his considerable learning about the supposed habits of sea-creatures:

The Shark with pointed Teeth is arm'd for Prey;
He breaks thro' all, and clears the liquid Way;
While the fond Sucking-fish (a harmless Breed)
With fastned Lips supply their daily need,
And with a Mouth unarm'd they clinging feed.
No Lovesick Nymph's, or wanton Triton's Kiss
Is half so lasting, or so close as his.
The Urchins are by Nature fenc'd around;
None dares approach; for with a Touch they wound.
Wrapt up within themselves they guarded lie,
And to their own Embrace for Safety fly.

Augustan pastoral must not be confused with two other contemporary genres in which natural description plays an essential part. The first of these is the topographical poem, in which description of a particular place is attended with suitable moral reflections. This type begins with *Cooper's Hill* by **Sir John Denham** (1615–69), and includes Pope's *Windsor Forest*, and *Grongar Hill* by **John Dyer** (1699–1758). Wordsworth's *Tintern Abbey* ultimately derives from this tradition. The second is the long descriptive poem, such as *The Seasons* by **James Thomson** (1700–48), deriving from Virgil's *Georgics*, of which the last notable example is *The Shepherd's Calendar* by **John Clare** (1793–1864). Nevertheless the new feeling for nature which the fashion for poems of these types evinced, affected the pastoral, ridding it of some of its formality. Another factor was the revival of interest in the ballad and in ballad metres.

Allan Ramsay (1686–1758) is of importance for the revival of Scottish vernacular poetry, and therefore as a forerunner of Burns. His pastoral drama *The Gentle Shepherd* contains the following well-known song:

My Peggy is a young thing,
Just enter'd in her teens,
Fair as the day, and sweet as May,

Fair as the day, and always gay.
My Peggy is a young thing,
And I'm not very auld,
Yet well I like to meet her at
The wauking of the fauld.

My Peggy speaks sae sweetly,
Whene'er we meet alane,
I wish nae mair to lay my care,
I wish nae mair of a' that's rare.
My Peggy speaks sae sweetly,
To all the lave I'm cauld;
But she gars a' my spirits glow
At wauking of the fauld.

My Peggy smiles sae kindly
Whene'er I whisper love,
That I look down on a' the town,
That I look down upon a crown.
My Peggy smiles sae kindly,
It makes me blyth and bauld;
And naething gi'es me sic delight
As wauking of the fauld.

My Peggy sings sae saftly
When on my pipe I play,
By a' the rest it is confest,
By a' the rest that she sings best.
My Peggy sings sae saftly,
And in her sangs are tald,
With innocence the wale of sense,
At wauking of the fauld.

Besides *The Gentle Shepherd*, Ramsay wrote a number of other pastoral poems, all occasional in character. They are really quite conventional, but the vernacular Scottish language, which was coming to be considered an equivalent to the Doric dialect of Theocritus, imparts a certain vigour and freshness to them. This can be curiously at odds with the real subject of the poem. Thus in the following extract, the two shepherds Richy and Sandy, lamenting for Addy, are none other than Sir Richard Steele and Alexander Pope mourning for the death of Addison. This passage refers to Addison's *Italy*, his *Campaign* and his opera *Rosamund*.

How sweet he sung where vines and myrtles grow,
Of wimbling waters that in Latium flow.

Titry the Mantuan herd, wha lang sinsyne,
Best sung on aeten reed the lover's pine,
Had he been to the fore now in our days,
Wi' Adie he had frankly dealt his bays.
As lang's the warld shall Amaryllis ken,
His Rosamund shall echo thro' the glen:
While on burn banks the yellow gowan grows,
Or wand'ring lambs rin bleating after ewes,
His fame shall last: last shall his song of weirs,
While British bairns brag of their bauld forbeairs.
We'll meikle miss his blyth and witty jest,
At spaining time, or at our Lambmass feast.
O' Richy! but 'tis hard that death aye reaves
Away the best fowk, and the ill anes leaves.
Hing down ye'r heads, ye hills, greet out ye springs,
Upon ye'r edge na mair the shepherd sings.

Among the poems of **William Shenstone** (1714–63), poet and land-scape gardener, is *A Pastoral Ballad*. It is written in the dactylic metre, and divided into two parts, *Absence* and *Hope*. This once very popular poet is a typical exponent of mid-eighteenth century sensibility. He is stylized and artificial, but can rise to a certain lyricism. We quote the opening lines of *Hope*:

My banks they are furnish'd with bees,
    Whose murmur invites one to sleep;
My grottos are shaded with trees,
    And my hills are white-over with sheep.
I seldom have met with a loss,
    Such health do my fountains bestow;
My fountains all border'd with moss,
    Where the hare-bells and violets grow.

Not a pine in my grove is there seen,
    But with tendrils of woodbine is bound:
Not a beech's more beautiful green,
    But a sweet-briar entwines it around.
Not my fields, in the prime of the year,
    More charms than my cattle unfold;
Not a brook that is limpid and clear,
    But it glitters with fishes of gold.

There is more freshness of observation in *Day, a Pastoral* by **John Cunningham** (1729–73). Cunningham was a strolling actor, who published a few poems; little is known about him. *Day*, divided into three sections, *Morning*, *Noon*, and *Evening*, is more akin to the descriptive genre, though on a miniature scale. His landscapes have something of the quality of a wood-cut by Bewick. We quote the opening lines of *Evening*:

> O'er the heath the heifer strays
>   Free; — (the furrow'd task is done)
> Now the village windows blaze,
>   Burnish'd by the setting sun.
>
> Now he sets behind the hill,
>   Sinking from a golden sky:
> Can the pencil's mimic skill
>   Copy the refulgent dye?
>
> Trudging as the plowmen go,
>   (To the smoaking hamlet bound)
> Giant-like their shadows grow,
>   Lengthen'd o'er the level ground.
>
> Where the rising forest spreads,
>   Shelter, for the lordly dome!
> To their high-built airy beds,
>   See the rooks returning home!

Hand-in-hand with the cult of natural sensibility, and like it, pointing the way to the Romantic movement, went the eighteenth-century taste for the oriental and the exotic. Pope, in the *Epistle to Arbuthnot*, refers to

> The Bard whom pilfer'd Pastorals renown,
> Who turns a Persian tale for half a Crown . . .

There was in fact a wide market for tales or poems presented as translations or imitations from oriental literature. *The Persian Eclogues* of **William Collins** (1721—59) belong to this class.

These eclogues were Collins's first published work, and were represented by him as translations:

I received them at the hands of a merchant, who had made it his business to enrich himself with the learning, as well as the silks and carpets of the Persians. The little information I could gather concerning their author, was, that his name was Muhamed, and that he was a native of Tauris.

It was in that city that he died of a distemper fatal in those parts, whilst he was engag'd in celebrating the victories of his favourite monarch, the Great Abbas. As to the eclogues themselves, they give a very just view of the miseries, and inconveniences, as well as the felicities that attend one of the finest countries in the East.

C

The time of the writing of them was probably in the beginning of Sha Sultan Hosseyn's reign, the successor of Sefi or Solyman the Second.

Whatever defects, as, I doubt not, there will be many, fall under the reader's observation, I hope his candour will incline him to make the following reflections:

That the works of Orientals contain many peculiarities, and that thro' defect of language few European translators can do them justice.

All this is of course a polite fiction. The poems are pretty, but conventional eighteenth-century work. They are four in number, accommodated respectively to morning, mid-day, evening, and midnight. Their Eastern colouring reflects Collins's reading in travel literature, but hardly any real knowledge of Persian poetry. We quote the opening lines of the mid-day eclogue, *Hassan: or, The Camel Driver*:

> In silent horror o'er the desart-waste
> The driver Hassan with his camels past.
> One cruise of water on his back he bore,
> And his light scrip contain'd a scanty store:
> A fan of painted feathers in his hand,
> To guard his shaded face from scorching sand.
> The sultry sun had gain'd the middle sky,
> And not a tree, and not an herb was nigh.
> The beasts, with pain, their dusty way pursue,
> Shrill roar'd the winds, and dreary was the view!
> With desp'rate sorrow wild'th' affrighted man
> Thrice sigh'd, thrice strook his breast, and thus began:
> *Sad was the hour, and luckless was the day,*
> *When first from Shiraz' walls I bent my way.*

Another example of the exotic is furnished by the *African Eclogues* of **Thomas Chatterton** (1752–70). These poems are among those which Chatterton wrote under his own name, and in normal English, apart from the pseudo-medieval pieces he attributed to an imaginary fifteenth-century monk called Thomas Rowley. The African Eclogues' idealization of African life should be read against the background of the anti-slavery agitation of which Chatterton's native Bristol was a centre. There are also three eclogues among the Rowley poems. The first of them is supposed to be a dialogue between two shepherds, recounting their miseries during the Wars of the Roses. The second gives a colourful and imaginative picture of Richard Coeur de Lion's crusading exploits. The third, in spite of its supposed medieval setting, seems to reflect some of Chatterton's revolutionary radicalism, though Sir Roger the priest has the last word:

Man. I rise with the sun,
Like him to drive the wain
And ere my work is done,
I sing a song or twain.
I follow the plough-tail,
With a long jub of ale.
But of the maidens, oh!
It needeth not to tell;
Sir Priest might not cry woe,
Could his bull do as well.
I dance the best heiedeygnes,
And foil the wisest feygnes.
On every saint's high-day
With the minstrel I am seen,
All a-footing it away
With maidens on the green.
But oh! I wish to be more great
In glory, tenure, and estate.

Sir Roger. Hast thou not seen a tree upon a hill,
Whose unlist branches reachen far to sight?
When furious tempests do the heavens fill,
It shaketh dire, in dole and much affright,
Whilst the poor floweret, humbly dight,
Standeth unhurt, unquashéd by the storm.
Such is the picte of life; the man of might
Is tempest-chafed, his woe great as his form;
Thyself, a floweret of a small account,
Wouldst harder feel the wind, as thou didst higher mount.

It may be proper to conclude this chapter with a brief note on **William Blake** (1757–1827). For Blake, the shepherd's life is a symbol of the state of the soul he called Innocence. Tharmas, one of his Four Zoas, is a shepherd in Eternity. The Zoas are the four gods who dwell in the human breast, and whose conflicts and divisions are the subject of Blake's so-called Prophetic Books. Tharmas seems to represent the sensuous part of man's nature, and is also connected with the Ocean.[1] *The Shepherd* from *Songs of Innocence* in its rhythm echoes Shenstone's *Pastoral Ballad*, a phrase or two of which also turns up in some of Blake's early poems. But we are now in a different imaginative world:

[1] I believe it possible that the character of Tharmas owes something to the Shepherd of the Ocean (Raleigh) in Spenser's *Colin Clout's Come Home Againe.* Blake's Miltonic borrowings and transpositions have often been noted by commentators, but his debt to Spenser still requires investigation.

How sweet is the Shepherd's sweet lot!
From the morn to the evening he strays;
He shall follow his sheep all the day,
And his tongue shall be filled with praise.

For he hears the lamb's innocent call,
And he hears the ewe's tender reply;
He is watchful while they are in peace,
For they know when their Shepherd is nigh.

5

Romantics, Victorians and Moderns

A reawakened feeling for nature, and a belief that imagery drawn from it was of special significance, was, of course, one of the leading features of the poetry of the Romantic movement. Nevertheless the formal pastoral had come to be associated with the artificiality of eighteenth-century poetry, and the Romantic poets in general reject it. **Wordsworth** (1770–1850) does indeed apply the term pastoral to some of his poems. But when he does so one feels that he is throwing down the gauntlet. He is implying a contrast between the realistic character of his own treatment of rural themes and the formalism of his predecessors. He is particularly apt to use the term when he wishes to emphasize the innocence and simplicity of country life. This is certainly the case with the *Pet Lamb*, which incidentally is of metrical interest, as being one of the few successful poems in English written throughout in Alexandrines:

> The dew was falling fast, the stars began to blink;
> I heard a voice; it said, 'Drink, pretty creature, drink!'
> And, looking o'er the hedge, before me I espied
> A snow-white mountain-lamb with a Maiden at its side.
>
> Nor sheep nor kine were near; the lamb was all alone,
> And by a slender cord was tethered to a stone;
> With one knee on the grass did the little Maiden kneel,
> While to that mountain-lamb she gave its evening meal.

In *The Idle Shepherd-boys or, Dungeon-Ghyll Force* Wordsworth observes a scene which clearly recalls to his mind parallels from classical pastoral poetry:

> Beneath a rock, upon the grass,
> Two boys are sitting in the sun;
> Their work, if any work they have,
> Is out of mind — or done.
> On pipes of sycamore they play
> The fragments of a Christmas hymn;
> Or with that plant which in our dale
> We call stag-horn, or fox's tail,

> Their rusty hats they trim:
> And thus, as happy as the day,
> Those Shepherds wear the time away.

Perhaps the finest of the poems to which Wordsworth applies the term pastoral is *Michael*. This may be considered as a narrative idyll, but its tone is tragic. It depicts the breakdown of the traditional pastoral way of life when the young man Michael leaves his home to seek his fortunes in the town. The ruined cottage and the uncompleted sheepfold are all that remain, as symbols of a way of life that has been destroyed.

Walter Savage Landor (1775–1864) is a classicist in the generation of the Romantics. His *Hellenics* are a series of idylls, mostly on mythological themes, very much in the manner of Theocritus. Some of them, such as *Chrysaor* and *The Last of Ulysses*, approach the epic style, while others like *Agammemnon and Iphigenia* resemble scenes from tragedy and suggest Landor's style in his prose *Imaginary Conversations*. *Silenus* perhaps comes closest to the world of pastoral. It opens as follows:

> Silenus, when he led the Satyrs home,
> Young Satyrs, tender-hooft and ruddy-horn'd,
> With Bacchus equal-aged, sat down sometimes
> Where softer herbs invited, then releast
> From fawn-skin pouch a well-compacted pipe,
> And sprinkled song with wisdom.

Adonais, by **Shelley** (1793–1822), his elegy on the death of Keats, though its imagery is not mainly pastoral, demands treatment here since it is a poem in the tradition of Moschus's *Lament for Bion*. This poem indeed provides *Adonais* with an epigraph, and is echoed in several places in the elegy itself. The name Adonais, we may note, is a variant form of Adonis.[1] The identification of the figure lamented with a nature-spirit, whose fate represents the annual death and re-birth of vegetation, which was implicit from the first in the form of the pastoral elegy, comes to the surface, as it were, in Shelley's use of neo-pagan mythological symbolism. Adonais is mourned by Urania. This goddess is, at one and the same time, the Heavenly Aphrodite of Plato's *Symposium*, and the Muse invoked by Milton, and by Shelley, as a personification of intellectual beauty. She leads a procession of other abstract figures, of natural powers like the Spring, and of personifications of Keats's own poems:

---

[1] The cult of Adonis was of oriental provenance, and had its original in that of the Sumero-Babylonian vegetation-god Thammuz, who was redeemed from the Underworld by his goddess-lover Ishtar. The name Adonis is semitic, meaning 'Lord'.

Where wert thou, mighty Mother, when he lay,
When thy Son lay, pierced by the shaft which flies
In darkness? where was lorn Urania
When Adonais died? With veiléd eyes,
'Mid listening Echoes, in her Paradise
She sate, while one, with soft enamoured breath,
Rekindled all the fading melodies,
With which, like flowers that mock the corse beneath,
He had adorned and hid the coming bulk of Death . . .

Oh, weep for Adonais! – The quick Dreams,
The passion-wingéd Ministers of thought,
Who were his flocks, whom near the living streams
Of his young spirit he fed, and whom he taught
The love which was its music, wander not, –
Wander no more, from kindling brain to brain,
But droop there, whence they sprung; and mourn their lot
Round the cold heart, where, after their sweet pain,
They ne'er will gather strength, or find a home again.

This mythological pageant is succeeded by a procession of human mourners. Shelley imagines Keats's contemporaries among the English poets as joining in the universal grief:

Thus ceased she: and the mountain shepherds came,
Their garlands sere, their magic mantles rent;
The Pilgrim of Eternity, whose fame
Over his living head like Heaven is bent,
An early but enduring monument,
Came, veiling all the lightnings of his song
In sorrow; from her wilds Ierne sent
Her sweetest lyrist of her saddest wrong,
And Love taught Grief to fall like music from his tongue.

Midst others of less note, came one frail Form,
A phantom among men; companionless
As the last cloud of an expiring storm
Whose thunder is its knell; he, as I guess,
Had gazed on Nature's naked loveliness,
Actaeon-like, and now he fled astray
With feeble steps o'er the world's wilderness,
And his own thoughts, along that rugged way,
Pursued, like raging hounds, their father and their prey.

The mountain shepherds are the Lake Poets – Wordsworth, Coleridge and Southey. The Pilgrim of Eternity is Byron (previously introduced as the Pythian of the Age, letting fly his shaft against the malignant critics).[2] Ierne's (i.e. Ireland's) sweetest lyrist is Tom Moore. The last, Actaeon-like figure, is Shelley's somewhat self-pitying and self-dramatizing projection of himself.

The spirit of Milton had been invoked earlier in the poem. *Lycidas* is clearly a model as well as Moschus's lament. Shelley's rather hysterical denunciation of the writer of the adverse review of *Endymion*, which he mistakenly supposed to have caused Keats's death, may be taken as the equivalent of St. Peter's speech in Milton's poem.

Like *Lycidas*, *Adonais* leads on to an apotheosis. This is not Christian but Platonic:

> He has outsoared the shadow of our night;
> Envy and calumny and hate and pain,
> And that unrest which men miscall delight,
> Can touch him not and torture not again;
> From the contagion of the world's slow strain
> He is secure, and now can never mourn
> A heart grown cold, a head grown gray in vain;
> Nor, when the spirit's self has ceased to burn,
> With sparkless ashes load an unlamented urn.

Shelley's Platonism, however, is not consistent. Elsewhere the thought is pantheistic and immanentist rather than transcendental:

> He is made one with Nature: there is heard
> His voice in all her music, from the moan
> Of thunder, to the song of night's sweet bird;
> He is a presence to be felt and known
> In darkness and in light, from herb and stone,
> Spreading itself where'er that Power may move
> Which has withdrawn his being to its own;
> Which wields the world with never-wearied love,
> Sustains it from beneath, and kindles it above.

Like *Lycidas* the poem concludes with a personal coda. But the tone is very different. It is oriented towards death, and indeed its imagery may seem uncannily prophetic of the actual manner of Shelley's own death:

> The breath whose might I have invoked in song
> Descends on me; my spirit's bark is driven,
> Far from the shore, far from the trembling throng
> Whose sails were never to the tempest given;

[2] The allusion is to Byron's satire *English Bards and Scotch Reviewers*.

> The massy earth and spheréd skies are riven!
> I am borne darkly, fearfully, afar;
> Whilst, burning through the inmost veil of Heaven,
> The soul of Adonais, like a star,
> Beacons from the abode where the Eternal are.

A very different poem of Shelley's is the early *Rosalind and Helen, a Modern Eclogue*. It is a dialogue between two women who meet on the shores of Lake Como, and recount to each other the highly distressing events of their lives. Both are victims of society's tyranny and superstition. The tone is that of the sentimental novels of the period. As a poem, this is about the least successful that Shelley ever wrote.

Passing from the generation of the Romantics to that of the Victorians, we find that the dominant poetic genres are the narrative idyll and the dramatic monologue. The first of these derives mainly, and the second partly, from the Theocritean tradition. Theocritus and Virgil were in fact two of the poets who most affected **Tennyson** (1809–92). We have already spoken of the derivation of the *Idylls of the King*. We should also consider in this connection his idylls on Greek mythological subjects, especially *Oenone*, and the poems in which he attempted to depict contemporary English rural life, such as *Dora*. These last really derive from Wordsworth's narratives, and those of Crabbe, but are very much inferior to both, being marred by sentimentality, which in such poems as *The May-Queen* degenerates into mawkishness. There is much more strength and reality in the poems, such as *The Northern Farmer*, which Tennyson wrote in the dialect of his native Lincolnshire. All this, however, bears only a marginal relation to the tradition we are considering. But in *The Princess* Tennyson does include a miniature exercise in the traditional eclogue form. It is described as 'a small Sweet Idyll':

> Come down, O maid, from yonder mountain height:
> What pleasure lives in height (the shepherd sang),
> In height and cold, the splendour of the hills?
> But cease to move so near the Heavens, and cease
> To glide a sunbeam by the blasted Pine,
> To sit a star upon the sparkling spire;
> And come, for Love is of the valley, come,
> For Love is of the valley, come thou down
> And find him; by the happy threshold, he,
> Or hand in hand with Plenty in the maize,
> Or red with spirted purple of the vats,
> Or foxlike in the vine; nor cares to walk

With Death and Morning on the silver horns,
Nor wilt thou snare him in the white ravine,
Nor find him dropt upon the firths of ice,
That huddling slant in furrow-cloven falls
To roll the torrent out of dusky doors:
But follow; let the torrent dance thee down
To find him in the valley; let the wild
Lean-headed Eagles yelp alone, and leave
The monstrous ledges there to slope, and spill
Their thousand wreaths of dangling water-smoke,
That like a broken purpose waste in air:
So waste not thou; but come; for all the vales
Await thee; azure pillars of the hearth
Arise to thee; the children call, and I
Thy shepherd pipe, and sweet is every sound,
Sweeter thy voice, but every sound is sweet;
Myriads of rivulets hurrying thro' the lawn,
The moan of doves in immemorial elms,
And murmuring of innumerable bees.

In the context of the long poem in which it is an inset, this eclogue is a plea to the Princess to abandon her intellectual pretensions and accept a domestic role.

Thyrsis by **Matthew Arnold** (1822–88) is a pastoral elegy on his friend and fellow poet Arthur Hugh Clough. Compared with *The Scholar Gypsy*, to which it refers, it is a somewhat unequal though moving poem. It is written in the same stanza as the earlier poem, which derives from that of Keats's Odes. To *Thyrsis* the criticism which Samuel Johnson made of *Lycidas*, might, one feels, with more justice be applied: 'We know that they never drove a field, and that they had no flocks to batten'. There is a clash in fact between the meticulous post-Wordsworthian observation of the real Oxfordshire countryside and the employment of a convention deriving from Theocritus. When the earlier poets employed this convention they created what was really a mythical world. Arnold, we realize, is vainly dallying with a false surmise. But the fact that he himself is aware of this gives to the poem its characteristic poignancy:

> Alack! for Corydon no rival now!
> But when Sicilian shepherds lost a mate,
>   Some good survivor with his flute would go,
> Piping a ditty sad for Bion's fate,
>   And cross the unpermitted ferry's flow,
>   And unbend Pluto's brow,

And make leap up with joy the beauteous head
   Of Proserpine, among whose crowned hair
   Are flowers, first open'd on Sicilian air;
And flute his friend, like Orpheus, from the dead.

O easy access to the hearer's grace,
   When Dorian shepherds sang to Proserpine!
      For she herself had trod Sicilian fields,
   She knew the Dorian water's gush divine,
      She knew each lily white which Enna yields,
         Each rose with blushing face;
   She loved the Dorian pipe, the Dorian strain.
      But ah, of our poor Thames she never heard!
      Her foot the Cumner cowslips never stirr'd;
And we should tease her with our plaint in vain.

The Dorset poet **William Barnes** (1801–86) wrote poems descriptive
of rural life in the dialect of his native county. Several of these are cast
in the form of eclogues. But though Barnes was a very learned writer
they are not at all literary, but realistic in tone. We quote from *The Best
Man in the Field*:

SAM.
You snub-nos'd flopperchops! I pitch'd so quick,
That thou dost know thou hadst a hardish job
To teäke in all the pitches off my pick;
An' dissèn zee me groun' en, nother, Bob.
An' thou bist stronger, thou dost think, than I?
Girt bandy-lags! I jist should like to try.
We'll goo, if thou dost like, an' jist zee which
Can heave the mwost, or car the biggest nitch.

BOB.
There, Sam, do meäke me zick to hear thy braggèn!
Why bissen strong enough to car a flagon.

SAM.
You grinnèn' fool! why I'd zet thee a-blowèn,
If thou wast wi' me vor a day a-mowèn.
I'd wear my cwoat, an' thou midst pull thy rags off,
An' then in half a zwath I'd mow thy lags off.

Barnes's work influenced that of another Dorset poet, **Thomas Hardy**
(1840–1928). Most of Hardy's work, both in verse and prose, is of

course pastoral, in the broad sense of the term. But it lies outside the convention in the limited sense we have been considering.

The Fleet Street Eclogues of **John Davidson** (1857–1909), a poet of the circle which formed the Rhymers' Club, are of some interest as employing the form to depict scenes of contemporary metropolitan life. *All-Hallows' Eve* begins with quite a telling description of the onset of a London Winter:

Brian: Tearfully sinks the pallid sun.
Menzies: Bring in the lamps: Autumn is done.
Percy: Nay, twilight silvers the flashing drops;
       And a whiter fall is behind.
Brian: And the wild east mouths the chimney-tops,
       The Pandean pipes of the wind.
Menzies: The dripping ivy drapes the walls;
       The drenched red creepers flare;
       And the draggled chestnut plumage falls
       In every park and square.

But it continues with a piece of fantasy in Menzies's description of Elfland:[3]

Menzies: In Elfland is no rest,
       But rumour and stir and endless woe
       Of the unfulfilled behest –
       The doleful yoke of the Elfin folk
       Since first the sun went west.

       The cates they eat and the wine they drink,
       Savourless nothings are;
       The hopes they cherish, the thoughts they think
       Are neither near nor far;
       And well they know they cannot go
       Even to a desert star:

       One planet is all their poor estate,
       Though a million systems roll;
       They are dogged and worried, early and late,
       As the demons nag a soul,
       By the moon and the sun, for they never can shun
       Time's tyrannous control.

[3] The Scottishly named Menzies is presumably the Scot Davidson. Does Percy, who believes that Elfland may be the ideal world, stand for his fellow member of the Rhymers' Club W. B. Yeats?

The haughty delicate style they keep
　　Only the blind can see;
On holy nights in the forest deep,
　　When they make high revelry
Under the moon, the dancing tune
　　Is the wind in the cypress tree . . .
　　.　　　.　　　.

But could you capture the elfin queen
　　Who once was Caesar's prize,
Daunt and gyve her with glances keen
　　Of unimpassioned eyes,
And hear unstirred her magic word,
　　And scorn her tears and sighs,

Lean would she seem at once, and old;
　　Her rosy mouth decayed;
Her heavy tresses of living gold,
　　All withered in the braid;
In your very sight the dew and the light
　　Of her eyes would parch and fade;

And she, the immortal phantom dame,
　　Would vanish from your ken;
For the fate of the elves is nearly the same
　　As the terrible fate of men:
To love; to rue: to be and pursue
　　A flickering wisp of the fen.

We realize that this is actually a description of the life of contemporary man. Davidson, a tragic and frustrated figure whose life ended in suicide, sometimes gives evidence of a more interesting mind, and one more capable of coming to grips with reality, than most of the rest of his poetic generation.

The *Echoes From Theocritus* of the clergyman and Winchester college-master **Edward Cracroft Lefroy** (1855–91) require passing mention here. They are not formal pastorals, but a series of sonnets, some based on passages in the Greek poet and some original. Lefroy owes something to Théophile Gautier and the French Parnassians, who aimed at a chiselled and objective style. He is at his best where the imagery is clearest, as in *At the Farm of Phrasidimus*; which is based on part of the seventh Idyll of Theocritus:

Where elm and poplar branch to branch have grown,
In cool deep shade the shepherds take their rest
On beds of fragrant vine-leaves newly strown,

73

Till the great sun declineth in the west.
From thorny thickets round, as if opprest
By secret care, the ring-dove maketh moan;
With sudden cry from some remoter nest
The nooning owlet hunts in dreams alone;
A merry noise the burnt cicalas make,
While honeyed horns are droning everywhere;
The fruit-trees bend as though foredoomed to break
With burden heavier than their strength can bear,
And if the faintest zephyr seem to shake,
Drop down an apple now, and now a pear.

A too easy use of the sonnet, with a tendency to employ it as a multi-purpose form, is characteristic of late-Victorian poetry.

Another, and much better known scholarly poet is **A. E. Housman** (1859–1936). The poems of *A Shropshire Lad* are not formal pastorals, but Housman's Shropshire is really a kind of imagined Arcadia. The following poem with its mythological allusion may demonstrate his relation to the tradition:

Look not in my eyes, for fear
  They mirror true the sight I see,
And there you find your face too clear
  And love it and be lost like me.
One the long nights through must lie
  Spent in star-defeated sighs,
But why should you as well as I
  Perish? gaze not in my eyes.

A Grecian lad, as I hear tell,
  One that many loved in vain,
Looked into a forest well
  And never looked away again.
There, when the turf in springtime flowers,
  With downward eye and gazes sad,
Stands amid the glancing showers
  A jonquil, not a Grecian lad.

It may come as something of a surprise to find that the formality of the eclogue convention has appealed to quite a number of poets in the twentieth century. In general, modern poetry has sat rather loosely to the traditional forms, and furthermore it evinced a reaction against the sentimental pastoralism (broadly speaking) of the so-called Georgian school, who flourished between 1910 and 1922. The manner of the

Georgian poets derived largely from that of Housman, and their view of the country was mainly an escapist one. We should except from this such a writer as **Edmund Blunden** (b. 1896) who writes more in the tradition of Hardy, and also **Edward Thomas** (1878–1917), whose work lies outside the Georgian ambience.

W. B. Yeats (1865–1939) in an early essay, published in *Ideas of Good and Evil* (1910), tells us how, as a boy, the two poets who most appealed to him were Spenser and Shelley; and how he tried to combine their styles in a pastoral play. Two passages from this play Yeats thought worthy of preservation, and they now stand at the beginning of his *Collected Poems*, as *The Song of the Sad Shepherd* and *The Happy Shepherd*. It should be realized, however, that Yeats continually revised, even to the point of re-writing, his early poems down to the end of his life. The opening of *The Song of the Happy Shepherd* prefigures some of Yeats's enduring themes and attitudes:

> The woods of Arcady are dead,
> And over is their antique joy;
> Of old the world on dreaming fed;
> Grey Truth is now her painted toy;
> Yet still she turns her restless head:
> But O, sick children of the world,
> Of all the many changing things
> In dreary dancing past us whirled,
> To the cracked tune that Chronos sings,
> Words alone are certain good.

There are echoes of Shelley's closing chorus to *Hellas*, which we have already quoted as deriving from Virgil's Messianic Eclogue, and which Yeats was later to adapt, with irony and bitterness, in his song from *The Resurrection*. But the end of the poem is closer to the world of the conventional pastoral:

> I must be gone: there is a grave
> Where daffodil and lily wave,
> And I would please the hapless faun,
> Buried under the sleepy ground,
> With mirthful songs before the dawn.
> His shouting days with mirth were crowned;
> And still I dream he treads the lawn,
> Walking ghostly in the dew,

> Pierced by my glad singing through,
> My songs of old earth's dreamy youth:
> But ah! she dreams not now; dream thou!
> For fair are poppies on the brow:
> Dream, dream, for this is also sooth.

Yeats returned to the pastoral in *Shepherd and Goatherd* published in *The Wild Swans at Coole* (1919), which is, in fact, a formal eclogue. This poem is really an elegy on Major Robert Gregory, killed in the First World War, and contains a tribute to Yeats's friend, Lady Gregory:

> She goes about her house erect and calm
> Between the pantry and the linen-chest,
> Or else at meadow or at grazing overlooks
> Her labouring men, as though her darling lived,
> But for her grandson now; there is no change
> But such as I have seen upon her face
> Watching our shepherd sports at harvest-time
> When her son's turn was over.

One of Yeats's last poems, *The Man and the Echo*, is also, in a sense, an allusion to the eclogue. The device of introducing an echo, which pertinently repeats the last words of the speaker, was a favourite with the poets of the seventeenth century. Webster introduces it in his tragedy *The Duchess of Malfi*, and it is parodied in a mock-pastoral by Swift. It may have been the latter poem which suggested the device to Yeats. *The Man and the Echo* is however deeply serious. In it we find the old poet facing the mystery which lies beyond death, and considering the question of his past responsibilities:

> *Man*
> Did that play of mine send out
> Certain men the English shot?
> Did words of mine put too great strain
> On that woman's reeling brain?
> Could my spoken words have checked
> That whereby a house lay wrecked?
> And all seems evil until I
> Sleepless would lie down and die.
>
> *Echo*
> Lie down and die.

The play alluded to is *Cathleen ni Hoolihan*, which helped to arouse the Irish Nationalist feeling which led to the rising of 1916.

An Idyll for Glaucus is the title of an early poem by **Ezra Pound** (b. 1885). It is a mythological idyll, somewhat reminiscent of Landor's *Hellenics*. The speaker is a girl supposed to be in love with Glaucus, who was transformed into a sea-god by eating a certain herb:

> Whither he went I may not come, it seems
> He is become estranged from all the rest,
> And all the sea is now his wonder-house.
> And he may sink unto strange depths, he tells me of,
> That have no light as we it deem.
> E'en now he speaks strange words. I did not know
> One half the substance of his speech with me.
> And then when I saw naught he sudden leaped,
> And shot, a gleam of silver, down, away.
> And I have spent three days upon this rock
> And yet he comes no more.
> He did not even seem to know
> I watched him gliding through the vitreous deep.

A Veld Eclogue: The Pioneers by the South African poet **Roy Campbell** (1902–57) is a satire on his fellow-countrymen, written in a pastiche of the Augustan style:

> On the bare veld where nothing ever grows
> Save beards and nails and blisters on the nose,
> Johnny and Piet, two simple shepherds, lay
> Watching their flock grow thinner every day –
> Their one joint Nanny-goat, poor trustful thing,
> That by the fence had waited since last spring
> Lest any of the stakes that there were stuck
> Should sprout a withered leaf for her to suck.
> Rough was the labour of those hardy swains,
> Sometimes they lay and waited for the rains,
> Sometimes with busy twigs they switched the flies
> Or paused to damn a passing nigger's eyes:
> Sometimes, as now, they peeled them off their hose
> And hacked the jiggers from their gnarly toes.
> At times they lay and watched their blisters heal,
> At others, sweated forth a scanty meal
> Prone on their backs between their Nanny's shins –
> After the manner of the Roman twins.

Campbell's *Jungle Eclogue* was written during the Second World War. In it two British N.C.O's, in the jungle, encounter a gigantic figure which reveals itself as the Nat, a personification of the malaria by which the poet himself was attacked. The poem contains some of Campbell's more violent and ill-judged satire, especially against left-wing intellectuals.

The socially-conscious poets of the nineteen-thirties also employed the eclogue form as a vehicle for irony and satire. An example is the early *Eclogue by a Five-Barred Gate*, by **W. H. Auden** (b. 1907). Auden also gives the title of 'A Modern Eclogue' to one of the longer poems of his later period, *The Age of Anxiety*. It is in fact a series of internal monologues. The characters meet casually in a New York bar, and later retire to the apartment of one of them, Rosetta.

The *Eclogue for Christmas* by **Louis MacNeice** (1907–63) is a typical poem of its period. Two not very clearly distinguished interlocutors, simply called A. and B., discuss the contemporary decline, but it concludes:

> A.   Let the saxophones and the xylophones
> And the cult of every technical excellence, the
>   miles of canvas in the galleries
> And the canvas of the rich man's yacht snapping and
>   tacking on the seas
> And the perfection of a grilled steak –
>
> B.   Let all these so ephemeral things
> Be somehow permanent like the swallow's tangent
>   wings:
> Goodbye to you, this day remember is Christmas,
>   this morn
> They say, interpret it your own way, Christ is born.

Goodman Jacksin and the Angel by **George Barker** (b. 1913) may be considered a kind of eclogue. It is a *débat* between a farmer and an angel, representing fallen man and his spirituality, the conflict between which is a persistent theme of this poet:

> Angel
> Thus, Goodman Jacksin, time has come
> For truth in cockleshells and nuts;
> I beg you leave your head and home,
> Come, cut the cackle, (cackle cuts)
> And to the catchpenny cosmos show
> The vipers nuzzling in your guts
> And my tall spectres shaped of snow.
>
> Jacksin
> What, get down off the five-barred star
> To let a bullying gale blow in?

I know what kind of a rogue you are,
When I step out, you will step in.
There are no matters, to my mind,
Worth any labour in the mouthing:
I'll just sit here on my behind –
All your wind amounts to nothing.

That pastoral imagery of a more traditional kind can still be used effectively is shown by the very beautiful *Shepherd and Shepherdess*, one of a group of love poems by **Norman Cameron** (1905–53), a poet whose rather small output has led to his being somewhat overlooked:

All day my sheep have mingled with yours. They strayed
Into your valley seeking a change of ground.
Held and bemused with what they and I had found,
Pastures and wonders, heedlessly I delayed.

Now it is late. The tracks leading home are steep,
The stars and landmarks in your country are strange.
How can I take my sheep back over the range?
Shepherdess, show me now where I may sleep.

The same may be said of the work of **William Bell** (1924–48), a poet of great promise who met an early death in a mountaineering accident. His first collection of poems, entitled *Elegies* (the only one published during his lifetime), consists of pieces cast in the eclogue form. He also wrote in *A Young Man's Song* a pastoral lyric which combines traditional convention with freshness:

Maidens who this burning May
Through the woods in quaint distress
Wander till you find your way,
Attend to what I have to say,
   But ask me nothing,
   Ask me nothing,
Ask me nothing you can guess.

Here I learned a year ago
This burden from a shepherdess:
'Love is wakefulness and woe;
'Where it hurts you ought to know.
   'So ask me nothing,
   'Ask me nothing,
'Ask me nothing you can guess'.

Said I 'when such as you complain
'You cry to courtesy for redress:
'Then may not I avenge your pain?'
But still she sang the same refrain,
  'Ask me nothing,
  'Ask me nothing,
'Ask me nothing you can guess'.

In that thicket where we hid
We found a primrose-bank to press,
And there I served her as she bid.
Let me shew you what we did!
  But ask me nothing,
  Ask me nothing,
Ask me nothing you can guess.

We have taken our trip through Arcadia. It is to be hoped that the reader has not felt himself unduly bothered by identical shepherds piping to identical sheep. The pastoral convention in fact shows itself to be capable of persistent vitality and considerable variety. Dr. Johnson's dismissal of it as 'Easy, vulgar, and therefore disgusting' was too sweeping. We ought also to consider C. S. Lewis's remark in *The Allegory of Love* on the sixth book of *The Faerie Queene*: 'Some readers cannot enjoy the shepherds because they know (or they say they know) that real country people are not more happy or more virtuous than any one else; but it would be tedious here to explain to them the many causes (reasons too) that have led humanity to symbolize by rural scenes and occupations a region in the mind which does exist and which should be visited often.' I hope that the foregoing pages may assist and encourage such visits.

Critical Books for Further Reading

GILBERT HIGHET, *The Classical Tradition*. Clarendon Press, 1949; O.U.P. paperback edition, 1957.

J. A. K. THOMSON, *Classical Influences on English Poetry*. Allen & Unwin, 1951.

HALLETT SMITH, *Elizabethan Poetry. A Study in Conventions, Meaning and Expression*. Harvard University Press, 1952 (distributed by O.U.P.).

W. W. GREG, *Pastoral Poetry and Pastoral Drama*. Sidgwick and Jackson, 1906; reprinted Russell and Russell, Inc., New York, 1959.

E. K. CHAMBERS, 'The English Pastoral' in *Sir Thomas Wyatt and Some Collected Studies*. Sidgwick & Jackson, 1933.

D. BUSH, *Mythology and the Renaissance Tradition in English Poetry*. University of Minnesota Press, Minneapolis, 1932.

M. Y. HUGHES, *Virgil and Spenser*. University of California Publications in English, 1929.

JAMES SUTHERLAND, *A Preface to Eighteenth Century Poetry*. Clarendon Press, 1948.

C. V. DEANE, *Aspects of Eighteenth Century Nature Poetry*. Blackwell, 1935.

H. GENOUY, *L'élément pastoral dans la Poésie narrative et le Drame en Angleterre de 1579 à 1640*. Paris, 1929.

Anthologies

E. K. CHAMBERS, ed. *English Pastorals, with an introduction*. London, 1895.

THOMAS P. HARRISON, JR., ed. *The Pastoral Elegy, an Anthology*. University of Texas, Austin, Texas, 1939.

E. K. RAND. *The Magical Art of Virgil*. Harvard University Press, 1931.

W. L. RENWICK, ed. *The Shepherd's Calendar*. Scholartis Press, London, 1930.

P. E. MCLANE *Spenser's 'Shepheardes Calender'*. Notre Dame University Press, 1961.

ROSEMARY SYFRET, ed. *Selections from Sidney's Arcadia*, with an introductory essay. Hutchinson, 1966.

C. A. PATRIDES, ed. *Milton's Lycidas: The Tradition and the Poem*. Holt, Rinehart and Winston, 1961.

ROSEMUND TUVE. *Images and Themes in Five Poems by Milton*. Harvard University Press, 1957.

ADINA FORSGREN. *John Gay, Poet 'Of a Lower Order.'* Natur och Kultur, Stockholm, 1964.

N. ROGERS. *Shelley at Work: A Critical Enquiry*. Clarendon Press, 1956.

LIONEL TRILLING. *Matthew Arnold*. Unwin University Books, 1939; 4th impression 1963.

Chronological List of Authors and Poems Quoted

THEOCRITUS (*c.* 316–*c.* 260 B.C.)
    from *Idyll* I (translated by C. S. Calverley)
    from *Idyll* III (translated by G. S. Fraser).

MOSCHUS (fl. *c.* 150 B.C.)
    from *The Lament for Bion* (translated by Andrew Lang).

VIRGIL (70–19 B.C.)
    from *Eclogue* I (translated by Dryden)
    from *Eclogue* X (translated by Shelley)
    from *Eclogue* IV (translated by C. S. Calverley).

LONGUS (? 3rd–5th century A.D.)
    from *Daphnis and Chloe* (translated by George Thornley).

ALCUIN (735–804)
    The Strife between Winter and Spring (translated by Helen Waddell).

ROBERT HENRYSON (1430?–1506)
    from *Robene and Makyne*.

ALEXANDER BARCLAY (1475?–1552)
    from *The Fifth Eclogue*.

BARNABY GOOGE (1504–94)
    from *The Eglogs*.
    from *Egloga Tertia*
    from *Egloga Secunda*

EDMUND SPENSER (1552?–99)
    from *The Shepheard's Calender*
        from *May*
        from *December*
        from *February*
        from *April*
        from *November*
        from *March*
    from *Daphnaida*
    from *Astrophel*
    from *The Faerie Queene* Book VI, Canto X.

SIR PHILIP SIDNEY (1554–86)
    from *The Countess of Pembroke's Arcadia*.

from *The Messiah*.

AMBROSE PHILLIPS (1675?–1749)
from *The Third Pastoral*.

JOHN GAY (1685–1732)
from *The Shepherd's Week*.
from *Tuesday; or, The Ditty*.
from *Friday; or, The Dirge*.
from *A Sober Eclogue*.
from *The Birth of the Squire*.

WILLIAM DIAPER (1685–1717)
from *Nereides, Eclogue Thirteen*.

ALLAN RAMSAY (1686–1758)
from *The Gentle Shepherd*.
from *Richy and Sandy*.

WILLIAM SHENSTONE (1714–63)
from *A Pastoral Ballad: Hope*.

JOHN CUNNINGHAM (1729–73)
from *Day, A Pastoral: Evening*.

WILLIAM COLLINS (1721–59)
from *The Persian Eclogues: Hassan; or, The Camel Driver*.

THOMAS CHATTERTON (1752–70)
from *The Third Eclogue*.

WILLIAM BLAKE (1757–1827)
The Shepherd.

WILLIAM WORDSWORTH (1770–1850)
from *The Pet Lamb*.
from *The Idle Shepherd-Boys*.

WALTER SAVAGE LANDOR (1775–1864)
from *Silenus*.

PERCY BYSSHE SHELLEY (1793–1822)
from *Closing Chorus from Hellas*.
from *Adonais*.

ALFRED LORD TENNYSON (1809–92)
'*Come down, O Maid*' (from *The Princess*).

MATTHEW ARNOLD (1822–88)
from *Thyrsis*.

WILLIAM BARNES (1801–86)
from *The Best Man in the Field*.

EDWARD CRACROFT LEFROY (1855–91).
At The Farm of Phrasidimus.

JOHN DAVIDSON (1857–1909)
 from *Fleet Street Eclogues: All Hallows' Eve.*
A. E. HOUSMAN (1859–1936)
 'Look not in my eyes, for fear'.
WILLIAM BUTLER YEATS (1865–1939)
 Song from *The Resurrection.*
 from *Song of the Happy Shepherd.*
 from *Shepherd and Goatherd.*
 from *The Man and the Echo.*
EZRA POUND (b. 1885)
 from *An idyll for Glaucus.*
ROY CAMPBELL (1903–57)
 from *A Veld Eclogue: The Pioneers.*
NORMAN CAMERON (1905–53)
 Shepherd and Shepherdess.
LOUIS MACNEICE (1907–63)
 from *An Eclogue for Christmas.*
GEORGE BARKER (b. 1913)
 from *Goodman Jacksin and the Angel.*
WILLIAM BELL (1924–48)
 A Young Man's Song.